THE INTROVERT ACTIVITY BOOK

DRAW IT, MAKE IT, WRITE IT
(BECAUSE YOU'D NEVER SAY IT OUT LOUD)

WRITTEN BY:

& Maureen "Marzi" Wilson

Adams Media
New York London Toronto Sydney New Delhi

Aadamsmedia

Adams Media
An Imprint of Simon & Schuster, Inc.
57 Littlefield Street
Avon, Massachusetts 02322

First Adams Media trade paperback edition NOVEMBER 2017

ADAMS MEDIA and colophon are trademarks of Simon & Schuster, Inc.

For information about special discounts for bulk purchases, please contact Simon & Schuster Special Sales at 1-866-506-1949 or business@simonandschuster.com.

The Simon & Schuster Speakers Bureau can bring authors to your live event. For more information or to book an event contact the Simon & Schuster Speakers Bureau at 1-866-248-3049 or visit our website at www.simonspeakers.com.

Interior design by Maureen Wilson

Interior illustrations by Maureen Wilson

Manufactured in the United States of America

10 9 8 7 6 5 4 3 2

ISBN 978-1-5072-0571-6

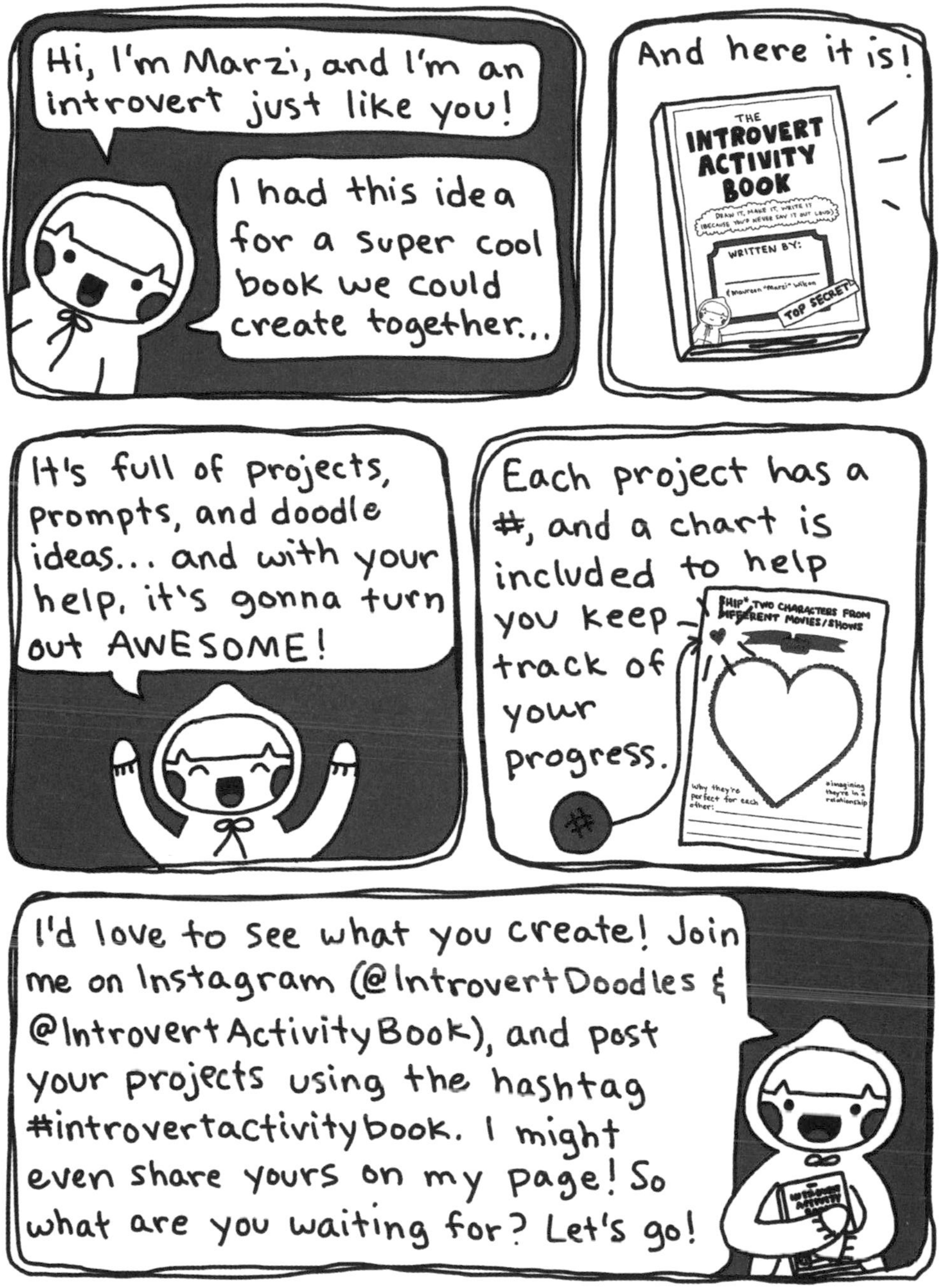
Hi, I'm Marzi, and I'm an introvert just like you!
I had this idea for a super cool book we could create together...
And here it is!
THE INTROVERT ACTIVITY BOOK
WRITTEN BY:
TOP SECRET!
It's full of projects, prompts, and doodle ideas... and with your help, it's gonna turn out AWESOME!
Each project has a #, and a chart is included to help you keep track of your progress.
I'd love to see what you create! Join me on Instagram (@IntrovertDoodles & @IntrovertActivityBook), and post your projects using the hashtag #introvertactivitybook. I might even share yours on my page! So what are you waiting for? Let's go!

PROGRESS CHART
complete in any order

#1 #2 #3
#4 #5 #6 #7 #8 #9 #10 #11 #12 #13
#14 #15 #16 #17 #18 #19 #20 #21 #22 #23
#24 #25 #26 #27 #28 #29 #30 #31 #32 #33
#34 #35 #36 #37 #38 #39 #40 #41 #42 #43
#44 #45 #46 #47 #48 #49 #50 #51 #52 #53
#54 #55 #56 #57 #58 #59 #60 #61 #62 #63
#64 #65 #66 #67 #68 #69 #70 #71 #72 #73
#74 #75 #76 #77 #78 #79 #80 #81 #82 #83
#84 #85 #86 #87 #88 #89 #90 #91 #92 #93
#94 #95 #96 #97 #98 #99 #100 #101 #102 #103
#104 #105 #106 #107 #108 #109 #110 Fill 'em in!

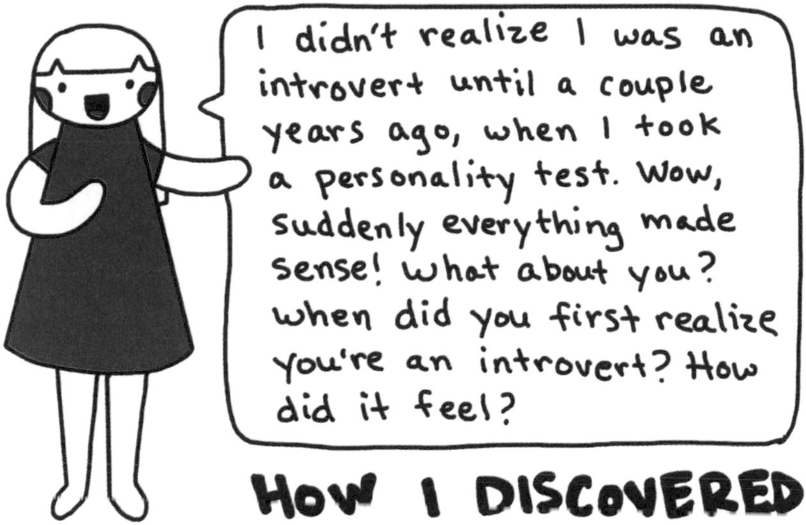
I didn't realize I was an introvert until a couple years ago, when I took a personality test. Wow, suddenly everything made sense! What about you? When did you first realize you're an introvert? How did it feel?

HOW I DISCOVERED I'M AN INTROVERT...

#1

Would you RATHER?

← circle your choices →

be kissed by an extended relative	or	be tickled by a stranger
have the ability to read minds	or	have the ability to become invisible
be able to fast-forward awkward moments	or	be able to pause happy moments
be interviewed live on the news	or	sing karaoke
learn you're a wizard	or	learn you're heir to the throne
lose your phone	or	lose your keys
have your library card revoked	or	get banned from your favorite restaurant
be called on to answer a question you don't understand	or	be tagged in a terrible photo
live without internet	or	live without privacy #2

WHAT SHOULD I DO TODAY?

ACTIVITY DICE

Cut on solid line →

Fold on dotted lines

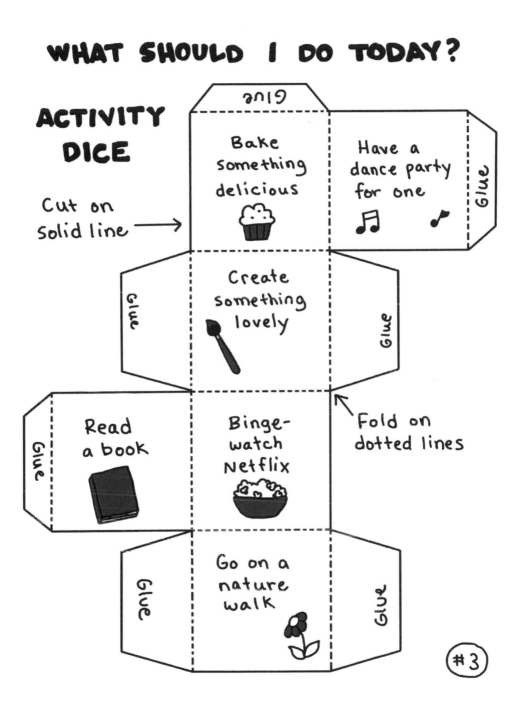

Glue

Bake something delicious

Have a dance party for one ♫ ♪

Glue

Glue

Create something lovely

Glue

Glue

Read a book

Binge-watch Netflix

Glue

Glue

Go on a nature walk

Glue

#3

WHY IS THIS PAGE HERE?

☐ Marzi forgot to draw something.

☐ You've been scammed into buying a book with blank pages!

☒ There's an activity on the other side that you've gotta cut out.

Whew! For a second there, I was worried it was the first one! Glad we got that straightened out!

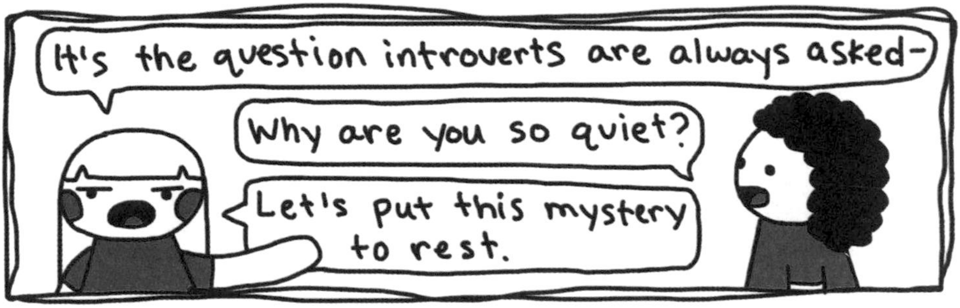
It's the question introverts are always asked-
Why are you so quiet?
Let's put this mystery to rest.

REASONS WHY I'M QUIET

Color this pie chart & the corresponding squares below.

Label the squares.

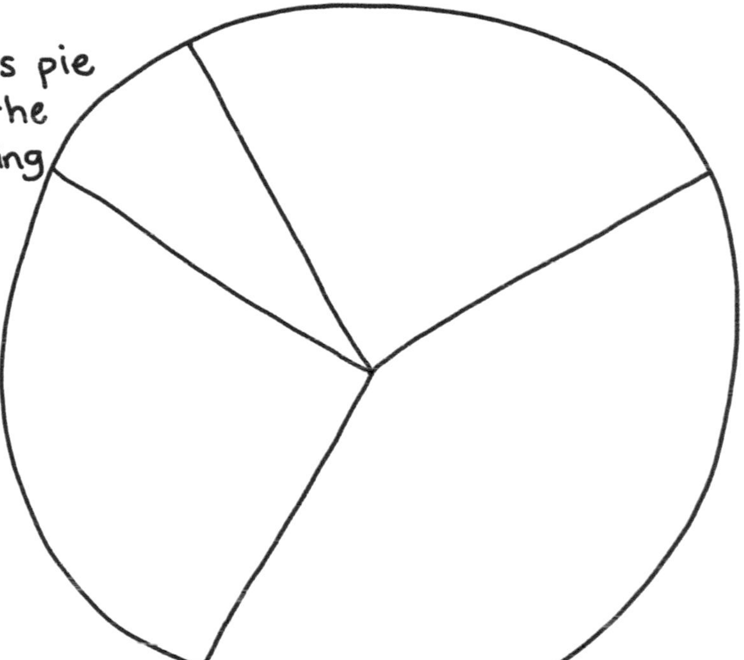

☐

☐

☐

☐

List ·of· Lasts

Last sentence in the book I'm reading:

NOM NOM

Last thing I ate:

Last thing that made me laugh:

Last text I received:

Last little, itty-bitty lie I told:

(PFFT, IT DIDN'T EVEN COUNT)

#5

BUDGET BAR GRAPH

Whatcha spending your extra pennies on?

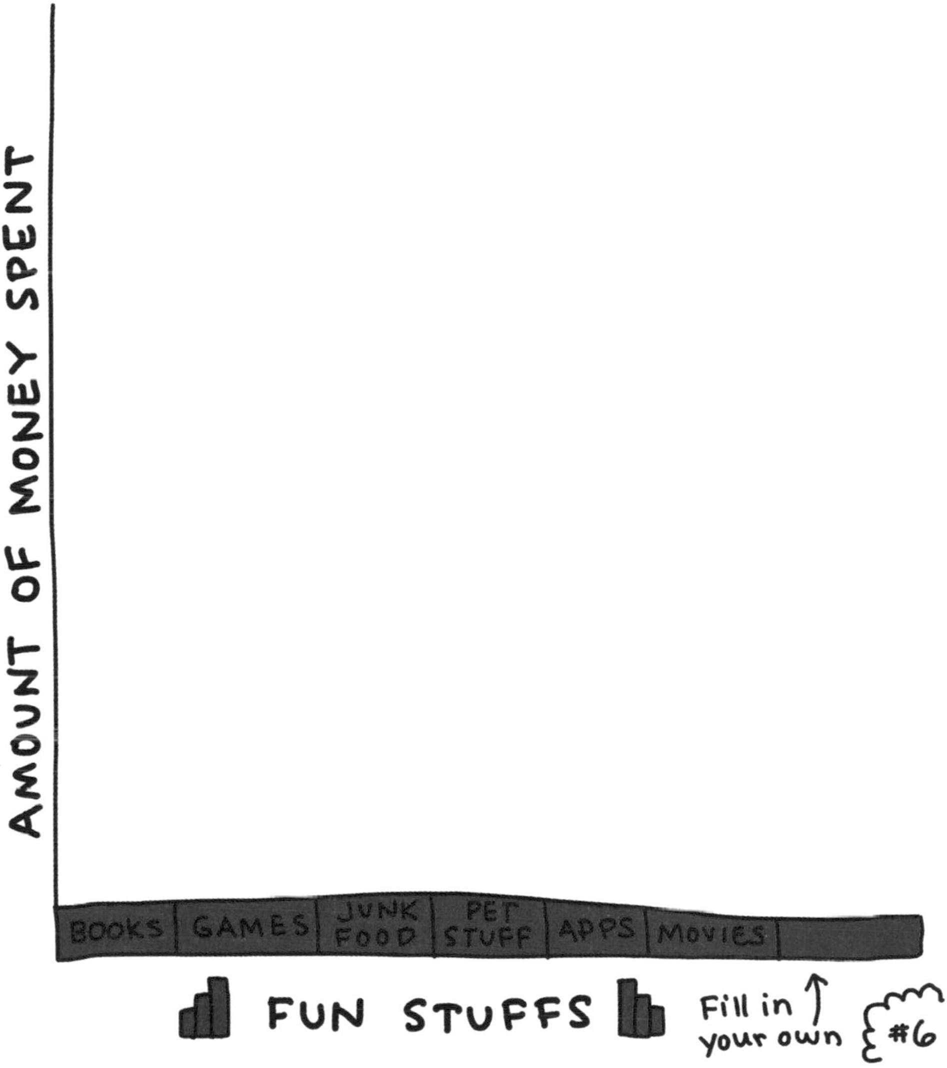
AMOUNT OF MONEY SPENT
BOOKS
GAMES
JUNK FOOD
PET STUFF
APPS
MOVIES
FUN STUFFS
Fill in your own
#6

INTROVERT MASCOTS

Withdraws into self when overwhelmed

Tough outer shell

Doesn't like to be rushed

Blends into surroundings

Gentle soul

Softie on the inside

Make your own!

#7

Weekend BUCKET LIST

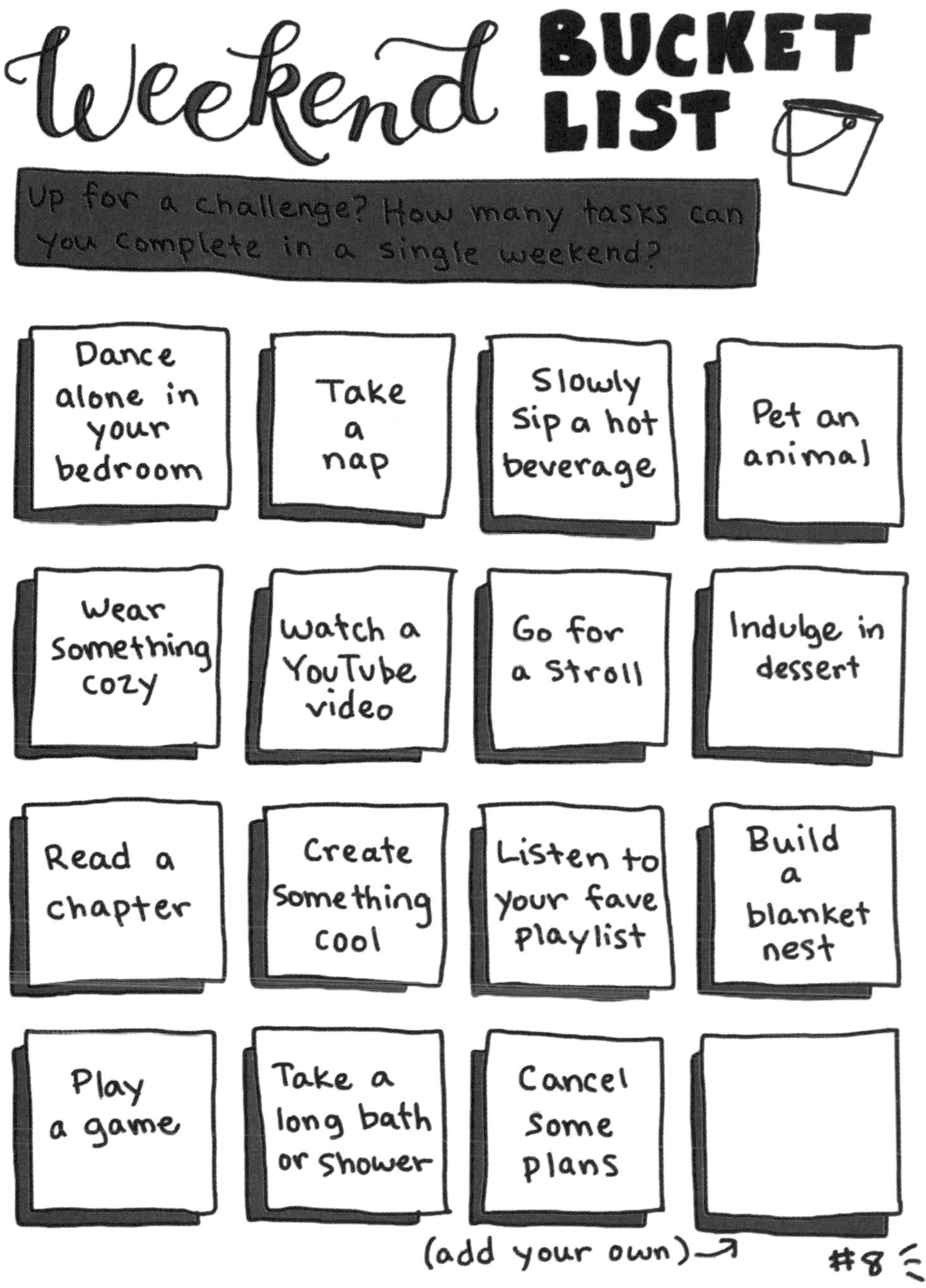

Up for a challenge? How many tasks can you complete in a single weekend?

Dance alone in your bedroom	Take a nap	Slowly sip a hot beverage	Pet an animal
Wear something cozy	Watch a YouTube video	Go for a stroll	Indulge in dessert
Read a chapter	Create something cool	Listen to your fave playlist	Build a blanket nest
Play a game	Take a long bath or shower	Cancel some plans	

(add your own) →

#8

Self-Care Quiz

FOR INTROVERTS

Self-care is necessary for introverts to recharge!
Circle your answers & turn the next page for results.

---

1 Which of the following best describes last night's sleep? **ZZZ**

   A) In bed by 10. Fresh sheets & sweet dreams!

   B) Lay awake for a couple hours, thinking about nothing and worrying about everything.

   C) Sleep? I don't understand, what is this "sleep" you speak of?

2 How much alone time have you had recently?

   A) Plenty! I'm refreshed and recharged!

   B) I've been able to squeeze a little in.

   C) Do bathroom breaks count? If so, 4.6 minutes.

3 Um... what's that smell?

   A) Probably my strawberry shampoo and eucalyptus bath bomb.

   B) Uh... my feet? I could use a shower.

   C) Failure. I. Am. Failing.

4. What's the funnest thing you've done lately?

A) I took the day off and played with art supplies/video games.

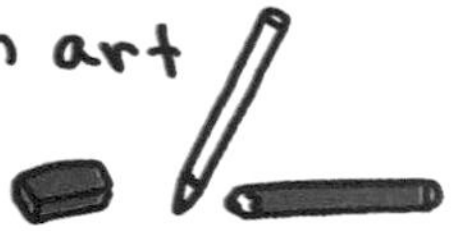

B) I read a book! (Okay, so it was actually my microwave's user manual, but still...)

C) It's a toss-up between doing my taxes and going to the dentist.

5. If your mama knew what you've been eating lately, what would she say?

A) You cooked that yourself?! I need the recipe!

B) Hm. What exactly is in that?

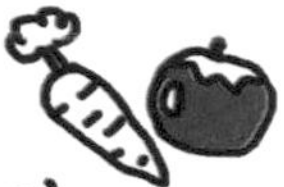

C) I raised you better than this. Eat a vegetable.

6. Describe your current stress level.

A) I'm totally chill. Going with the flow.

B) I'm going through a bit of a stormy patch.

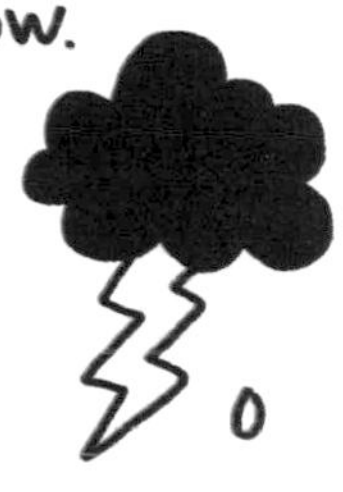

C) I'M DROWNING.

TALLY YOUR RESPONSES & TURN THE PAGE

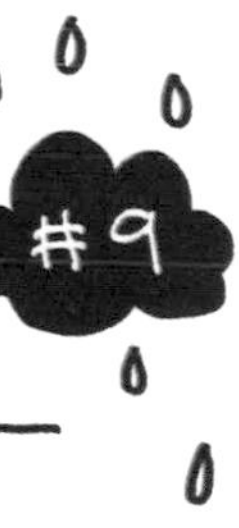
#9

A's _____ B's _____ C's _____

Mostly A's

GREEN LIGHT

You go! You recognize the importance of downtime, and make it a priority. You understand that focusing on self-care results in a happier, healthier you. Keep it up!

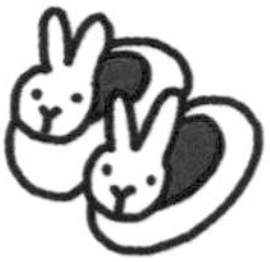

Mostly B's

YELLOW LIGHT

Better slow down! It's challenging to make time for self-care when life gets in the way, but taking time to recharge means you'll have more energy to tackle your to-do list.

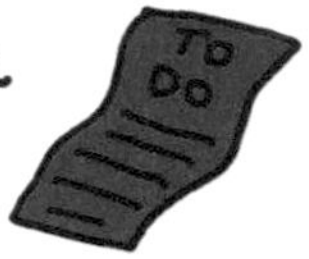
TO DO

Mostly C's

RED LIGHT

Stop. Breathe. Things have gotten a little out of hand, and it's time to regroup. Remember, rest isn't a luxury for introverts, it's a necessity! Do something kind for yourself today.

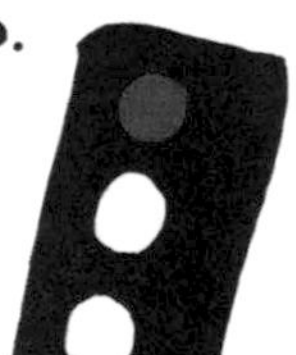

WHEN I WAS LITTLE, I BELIEVED...

I believed I could hatch an egg from the grocery store and have my own pet chick! I wrapped an egg in a washcloth and carried it around in my fanny pack for two weeks, until an unfortunate accident on the monkeybars put a sudden end to my experiment. What's something you believed?

- -

- -

- -

- -

- -

- -

- -

#10

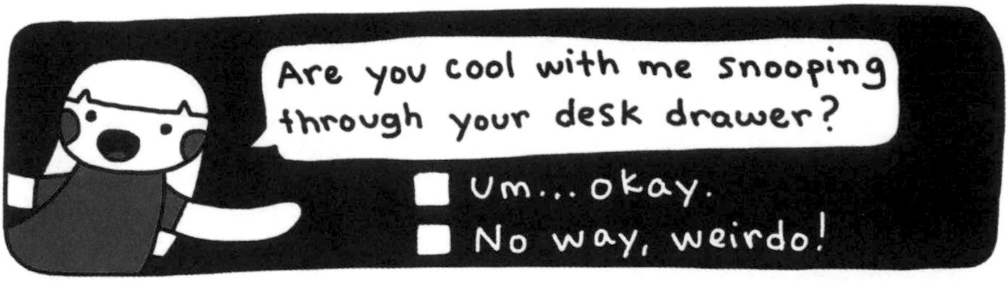
Are you cool with me snooping through your desk drawer?
Um... okay.
No way, weirdo!

TRACE THE STUFF IN YOUR DRAWER

#11

LET'S PLAY
Introvert
BINGO!

Mark off the squares that apply to you. #12
Get 5 in a row to win!

I order almost everything online.	I can't wait to be alone.	I spend most evenings at home.	Binge-watching is one of my hobbies.	I notice things most people overlook.
I still build blanket forts.	I keep my phone on silent.	I prefer animals over people.	I often feel misunderstood.	I'm super creative.
I'd rather have one best friend than a lot of buddies.	I'm better at listening than talking.	HOME   FREE	I'd rather be at the library than a club.	I dislike crowds.
I often get lost in thought.	Books make me happy.	I dread most parties.	I always text instead of calling.	I make up stories in my head.
my dream is to work from home.	I'm comfortable with silence.	I live for naptime.	I've made some of my closest friends online.	I become invested in the lives of fictional characters.

INTROVERT DREAM HOUSE

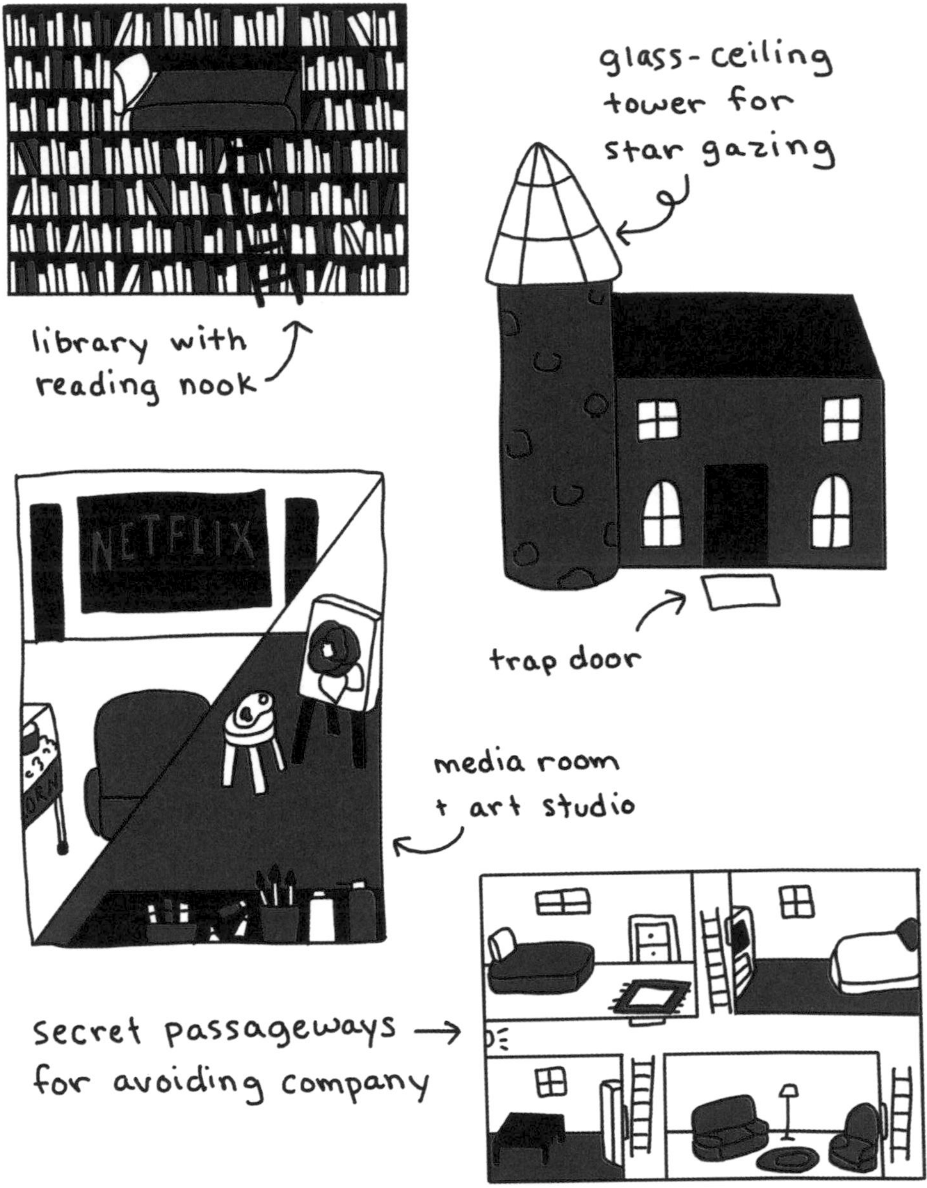
library with reading nook
glass-ceiling tower for star gazing
trap door
NETFLIX
media room + art studio
secret passageways for avoiding company

WHAT'S IN YOUR Dream HOUSE?

#13

A LITTLE BIT SENSITIVE?

Introverts are thought to be more sensitive to external stimuli. Would you say that's true for you? Circle the things you're sensitive to.

noise

sour foods

temperature

motion

light

odors

spicy foods

#14

when I don't get enough alone time, I feel physically exhausted. My battery is drained! What about you?

WHEN I DON'T GET ENOUGH ALONE TIME...

#15

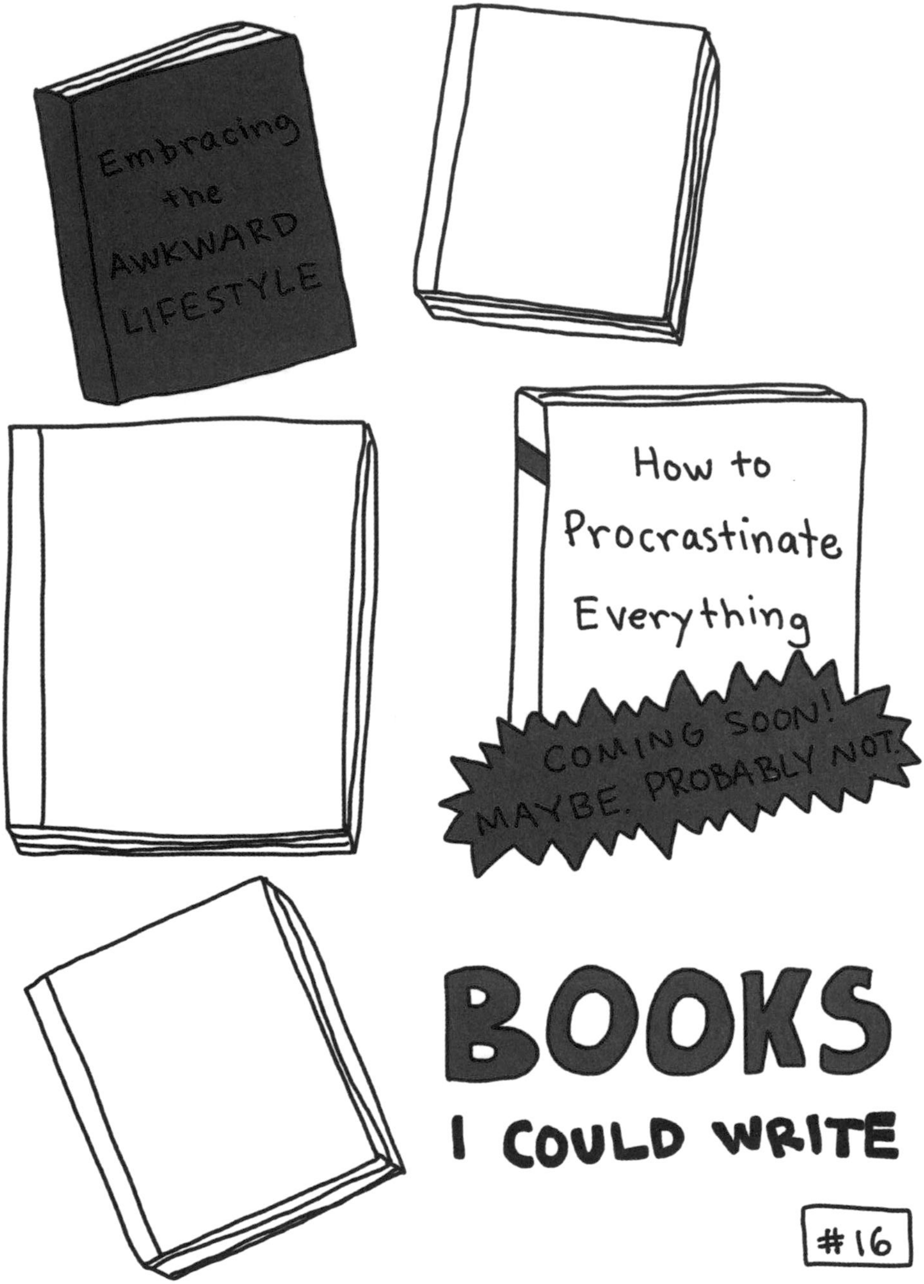
Embracing the AWKWARD LIFESTYLE
How to Procrastinate Everything
COMING SOON! MAYBE. PROBABLY NOT.
BOOKS
I COULD WRITE
#16

(NONE OF YOUR) BUSINESS CARDS*

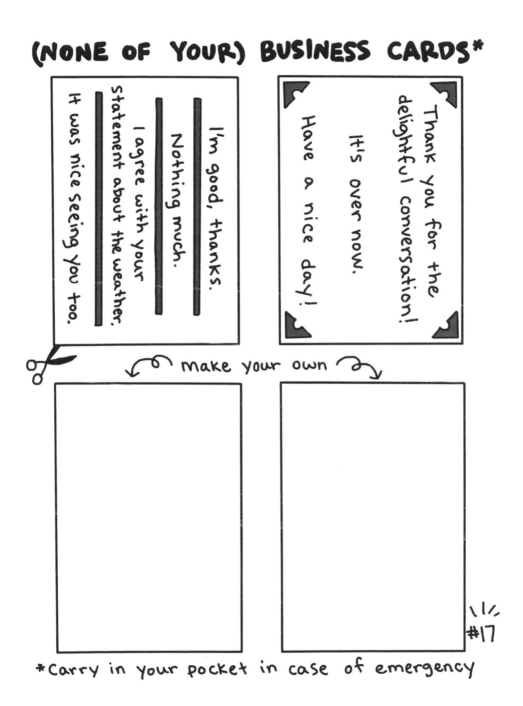

Thank you for the delightful conversation!

It's over now.

Have a nice day!

I'm good, thanks.

Nothing much.

I agree with your statement about the weather.

It was nice seeing you too.

make your own

#17

*Carry in your pocket in case of emergency

THIS PAGE IS <u>INTENTIONALLY</u> <u>BLANK</u>.

SO DON'T FREAK OUT ABOUT IT, OKAY?

SHIP* TWO CHARACTERS FROM DIFFERENT MOVIES/SHOWS

loves

*imagining they're in a relationship

Why they're perfect for each other: _____

_____

_____ #18

I'M SCARED OF...
CHECK ALL THAT APPLY

- clowns
- heights
- no wi-fi
- visitors
- deep water
- germs
- spiders
- crowds
- my bank account
- the dark
- public speaking
- blood
- dentists
- dogs
- being called on

- doctors
- ghosts
- small spaces
- needles
- phone calls
- bees
- commitment
- lightning / thunder
- ordering in restaurants
- snakes
- being an adult
- dropping my phone
- public bathrooms
- judgment
- flying

#19

Introverts know...

THE BEST GAMES ARE 1-PLAYER

- Take 5 shots with a rubber band from 4 ft
- Tally your score to win a cool [imaginary] prize!

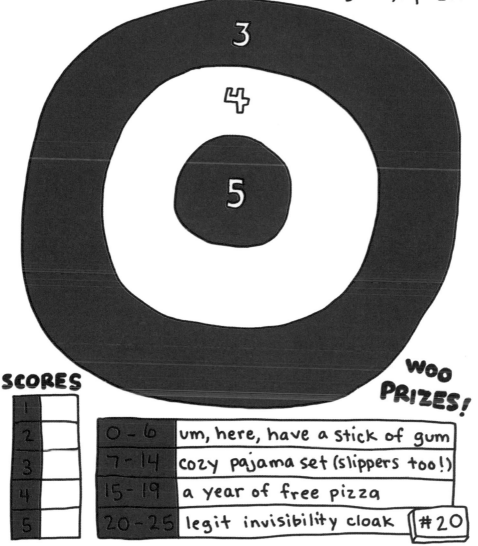

SCORES

1	
2	
3	
4	
5	

WOO PRIZES!

0 - 6	um, here, have a stick of gum
7 - 14	cozy pajama set (slippers too!)
15 - 19	a year of free pizza
20 - 25	legit invisibility cloak

#20

Love It -OR- HATE IT?

PLACES EDITION

COLOR THE ♡ OR THE 💔

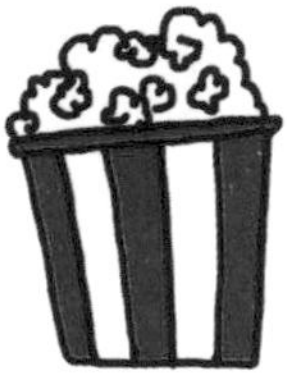

movie theater

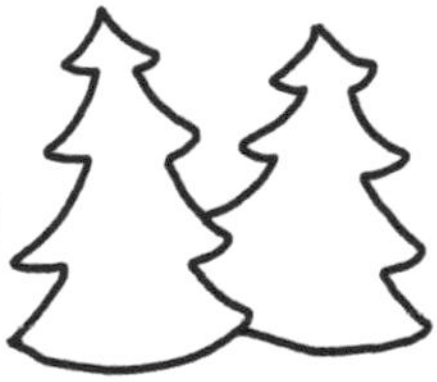

the woods

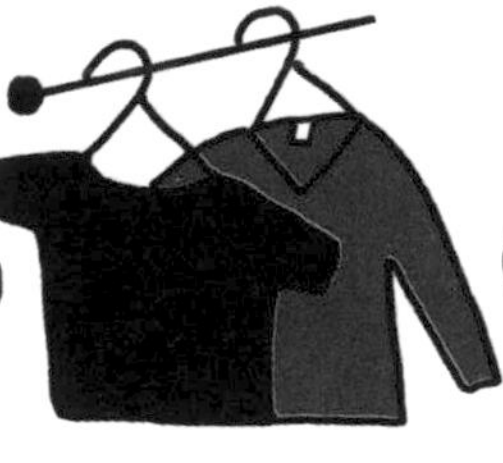

thrift store

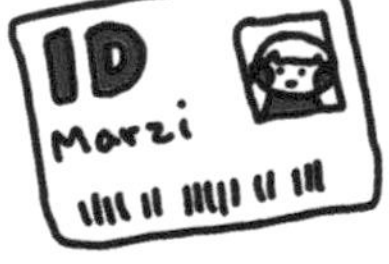
ID
Marzi

where I work or go to school

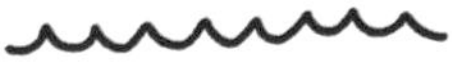

swimming pool

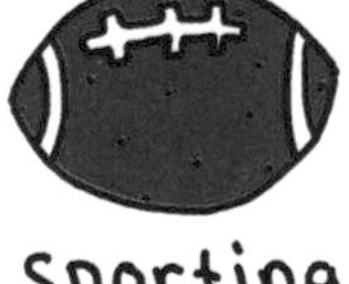

sporting events

#21

IF I WERE ASKED TO EXPLAIN

INTROVERSION, I'D SAY...

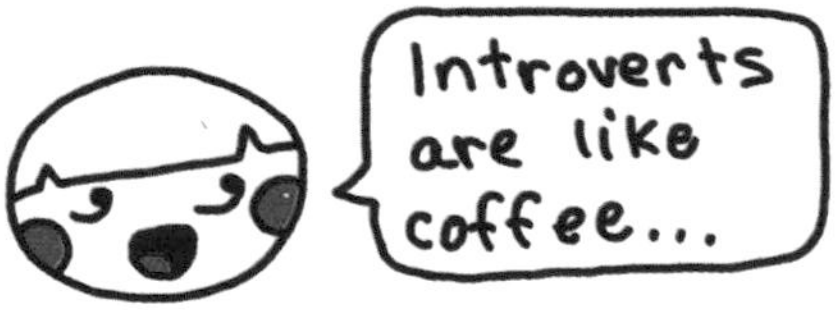
Introverts are like coffee...

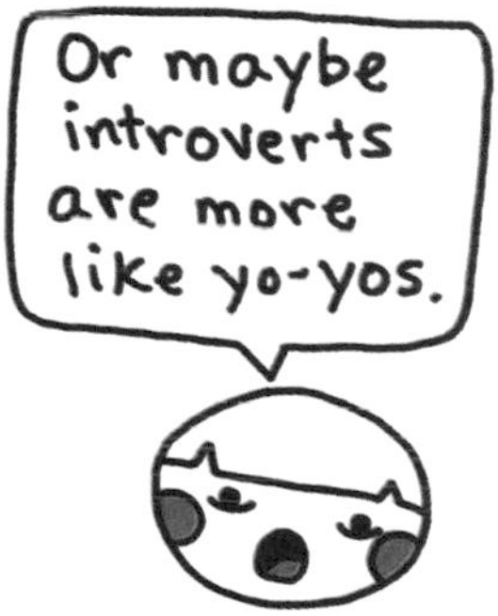
Or maybe introverts are more like yo-yos.

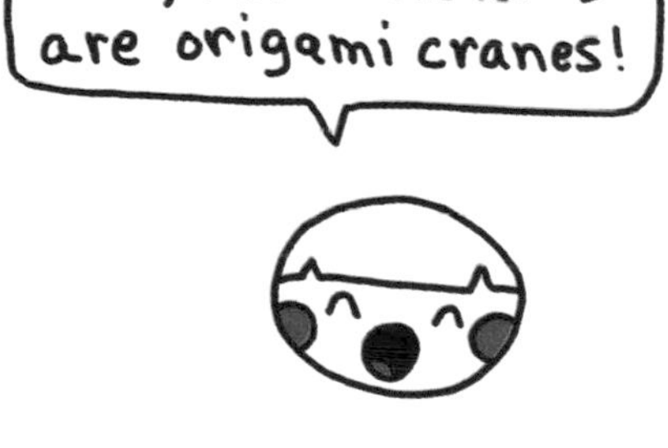
Wait, no! Introverts are origami cranes!

#22

THIS IS MY *favorite* COLOR

ITEMS THAT ARE MY FAVE COLOR

Doodle

Circle

It's always been my favorite. — Y or N

I'd paint my bedroom this color. — Y or N

I'd wear shoes this hue. — Y or N

I'd like a car this color. — Y or N

I'd dye my hair this shade. — Y or N

#23

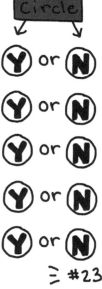

TELL ABOUT A

MOMENT

YOU'D LIKE TO

BOTTLE

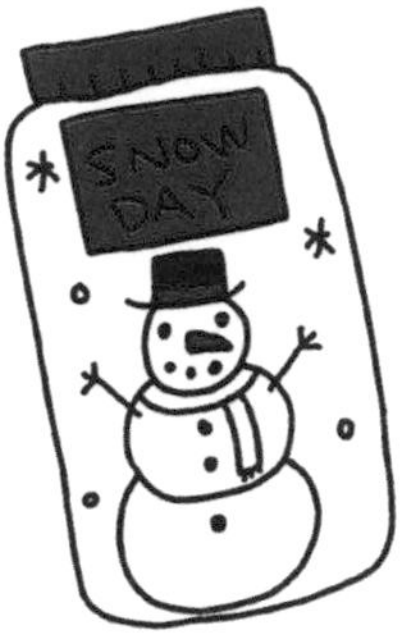
SNOW DAY

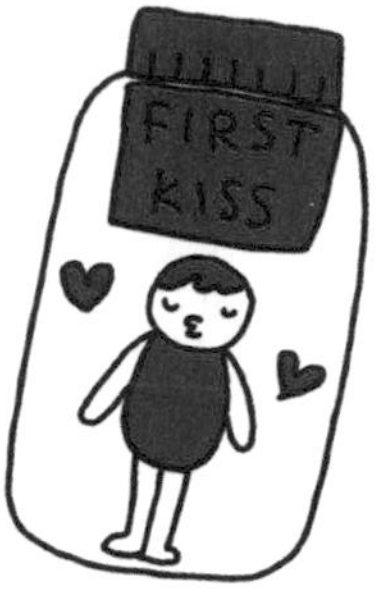
FIRST KISS

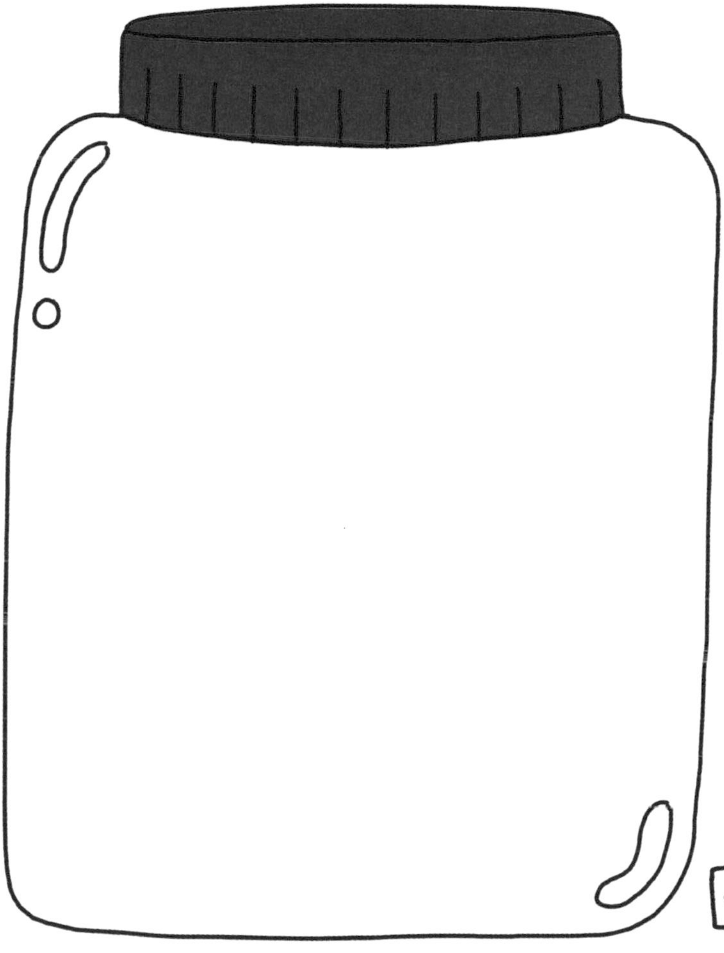

#24

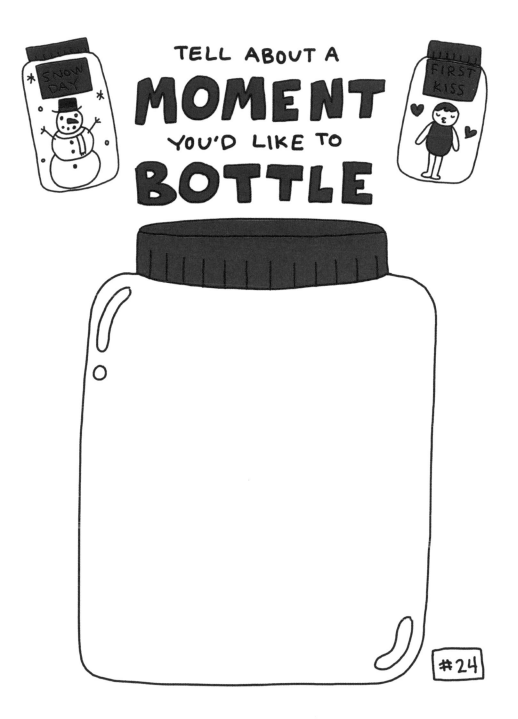

Introverts often have BIG imaginations!
We're visionaries. We're dreamers. We're gazers.

CLOUD GAZING

Draw today's cloudscape.

Do you see any shapes?

#25

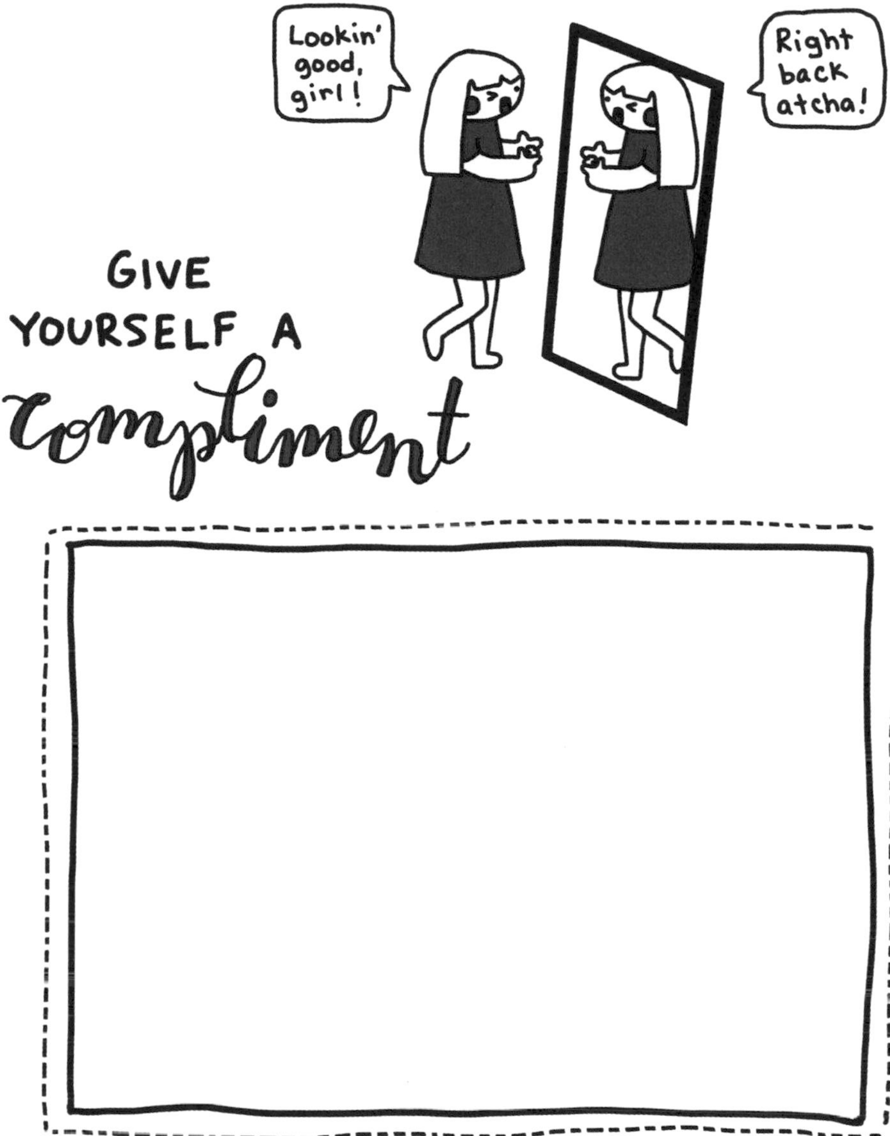
Lookin' good, girl!
Right back atcha!

GIVE YOURSELF A *compliment*

CUT IT OUT & HANG ON THE FRIDGE. YES, SERIOUSLY. GO!

#26

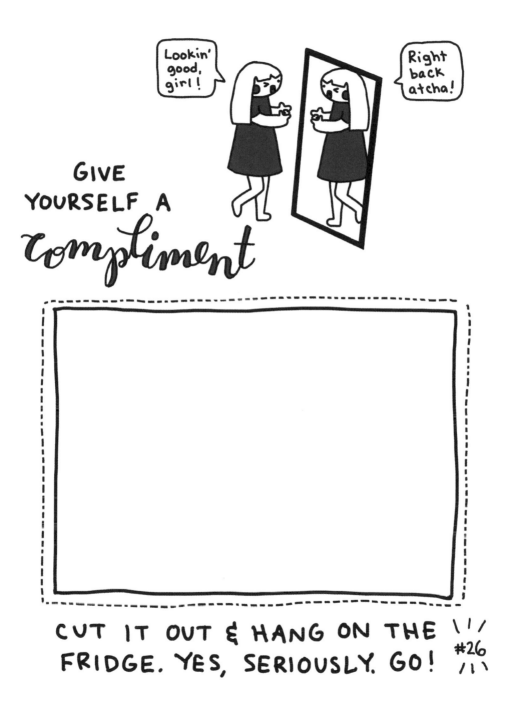

my mind during
small talk

BLANK

this page
(activity on reverse)

(((SOUND)))
Scavenger Hunt

Observation is an introvert's super power!
See how many of these sounds you can find.

birdsong	Siren	running water
ticking	laughter	tapping
music	thumping	phone ringing
an echo	whispering	- total - SILENCE

#27

WORD SEARCH

peaceful	silent
quiet	cozy	serene	zen
cuddly	solitary	tranquil	still
restful	comfortable	hushed	calm

```
G E R I O T W Y J D A Y T
C P L U F T S E R G R Z U
M O I V E D K D M A B O Q
L F A P H G I B T F P C I
E T R A N Q U I L N O G W
U V Z Y M O L E E M R O Y
L T W H R O R Z F D U L P
E C N T S L A O U T D R S
I J B E L S R V D D N G R
C A N I L T N Q U I E T W
Q U T C A I N C X R B J E
P S O B C D S C A L M D T
J H L U F E C A E P S I U
V E W S E R E N E H A Y Z
T W L M J Y X R M T N L Y
D E H S U H W L C Y Q U K
```

#28

Introverts can be fantastic leaders! They tend to be more cautious when making decisions, relying on research and thoughtfully considering multiple solutions. What changes would you implement if you were in charge?

IF I WERE PRESIDENT

INTROVERTS LIKE TO CONSIDER
WHAT'S BEHIND AND UNDERNEATH.

30

PLACE AN OBJECT OFF TO THE SIDE AND
TRACE THE SHADOW THAT FALLS ON THIS PAGE.

My Wish List

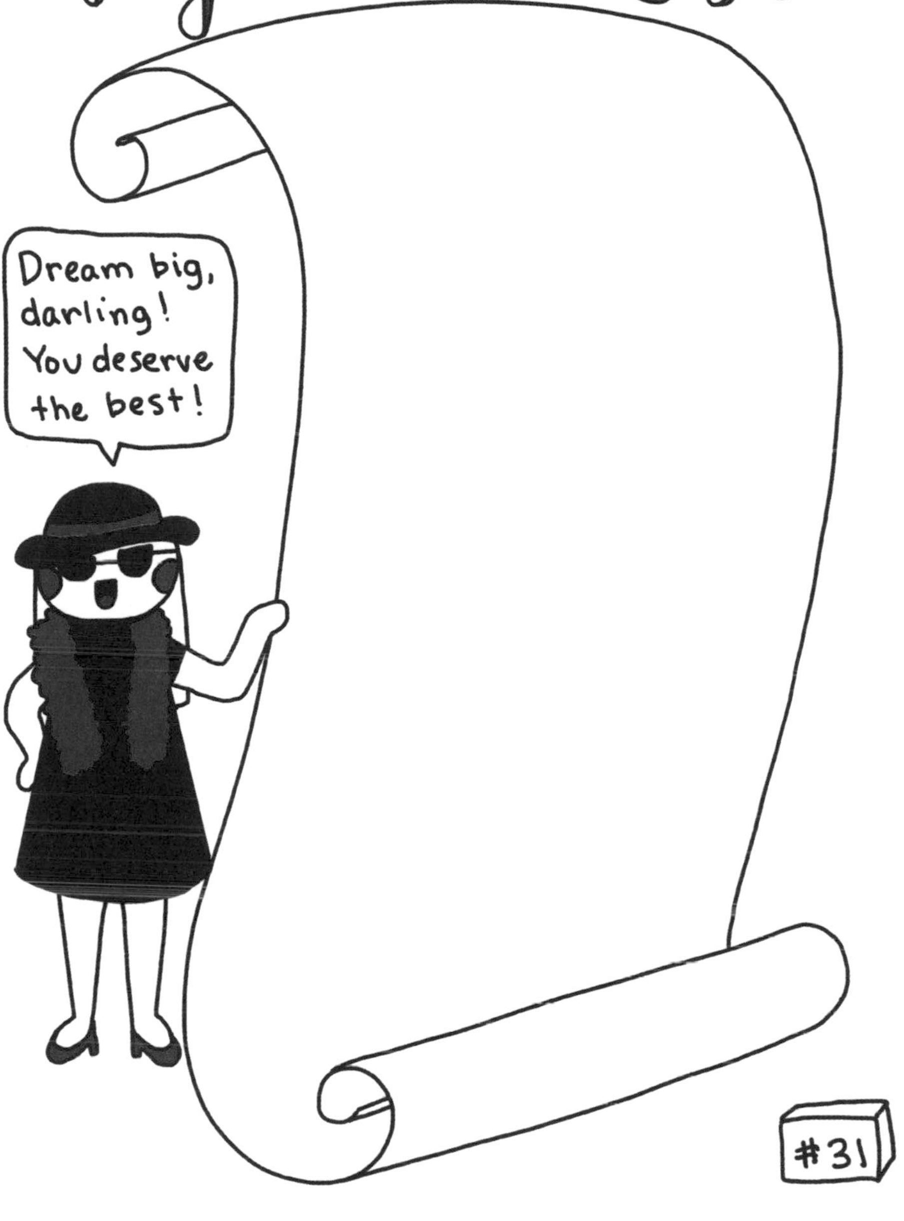

STUFF I'M GREAT AT

Pure AWESOMENESS!

Not to brag, but...
I'm kind of a
ROCKSTAR!

#32

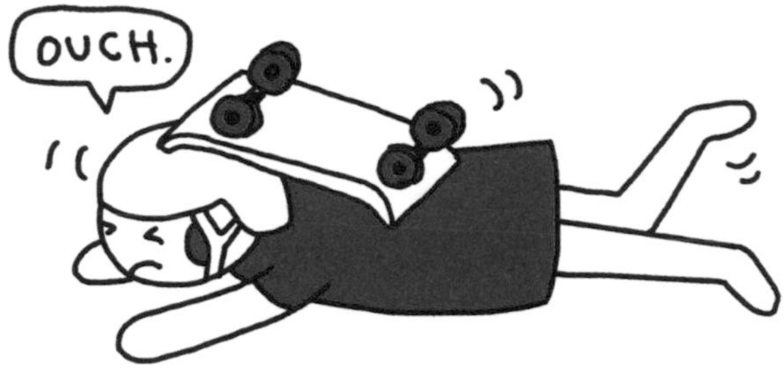
OUCH.

...AND A FEW THINGS I'M NOT SO GREAT AT

OH WELL

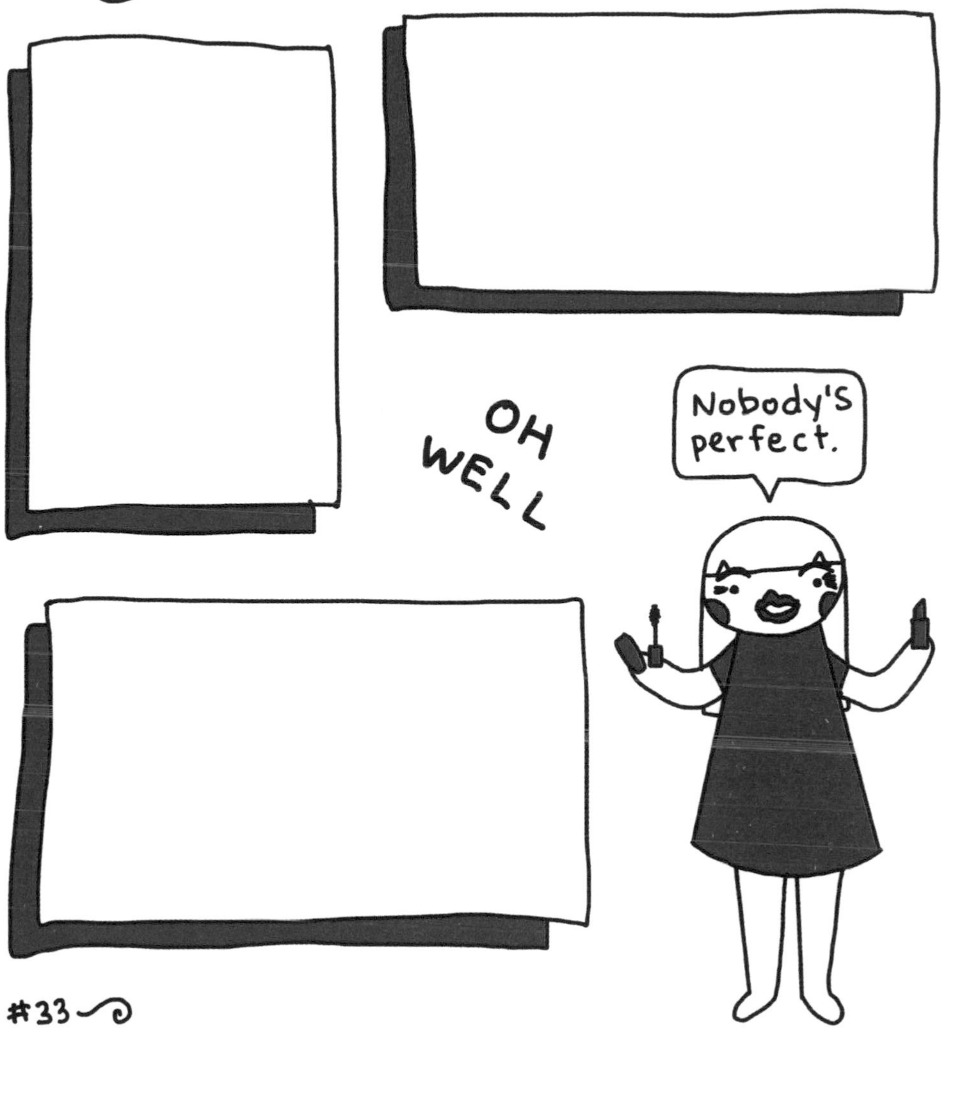
Nobody's perfect.

#33

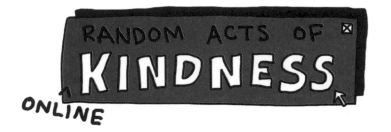

RANDOM ACTS OF ONLINE KINDNESS

- ☐ Compliment someone on their avatar
- ☐ Repost/retweet someone's meme
- ☐ Like a post that TBH isn't that great
- ☐ Share a link to a small blog
- ☐ Leave a supportive comment on a YouTube video
- ☐ Take the time to answer a question
- ☐ Find something nice to say about a beginner's artwork
- ☐ Leave a glowing review on a business page

#34

GOOD DEED FOR THE DAY ☑

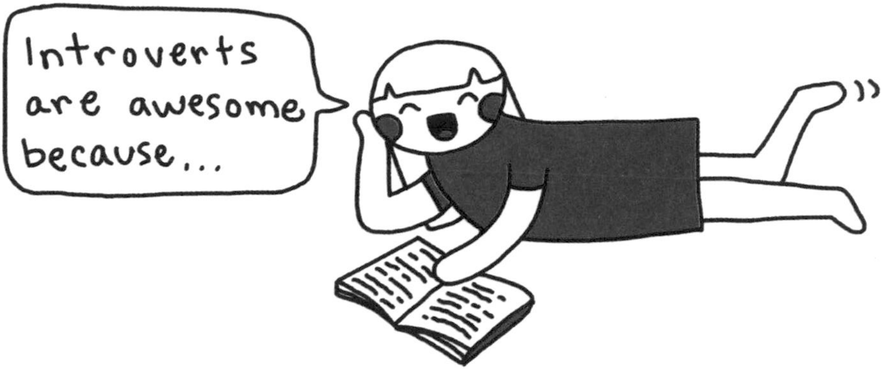
Introverts are awesome because...

#35

SUPER COOL

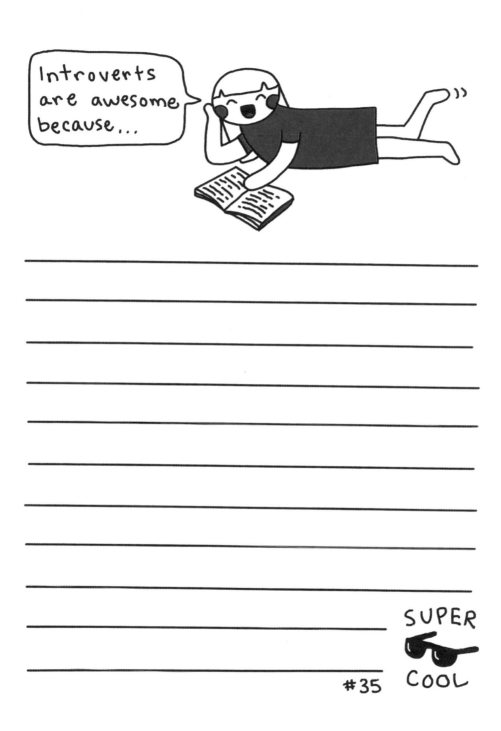

Introverts are notorious over-thinkers.
What do you wonder about in the shower?

SHOWER THOUGHTS

#36

Introverts are known for being observant, for noticing what others may overlook.

Find something small that's uniquely lovely, and leave this frame around it.

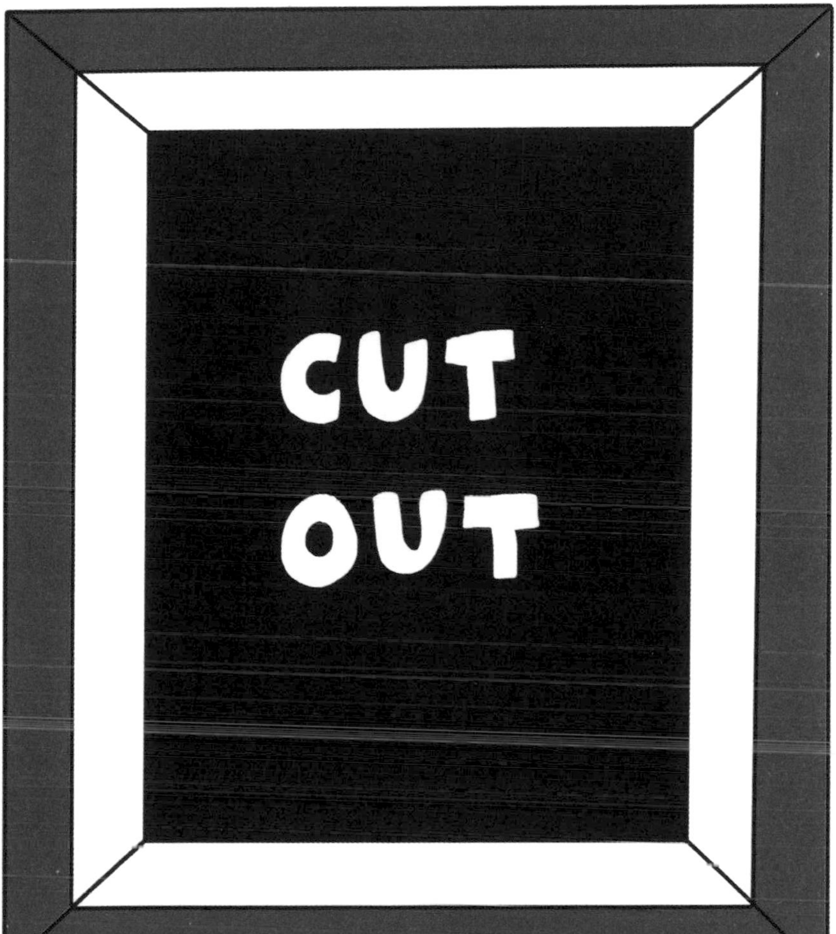
CUT
OUT

↱cut around outer line

#37

THIS PAGE LEFT BLANK

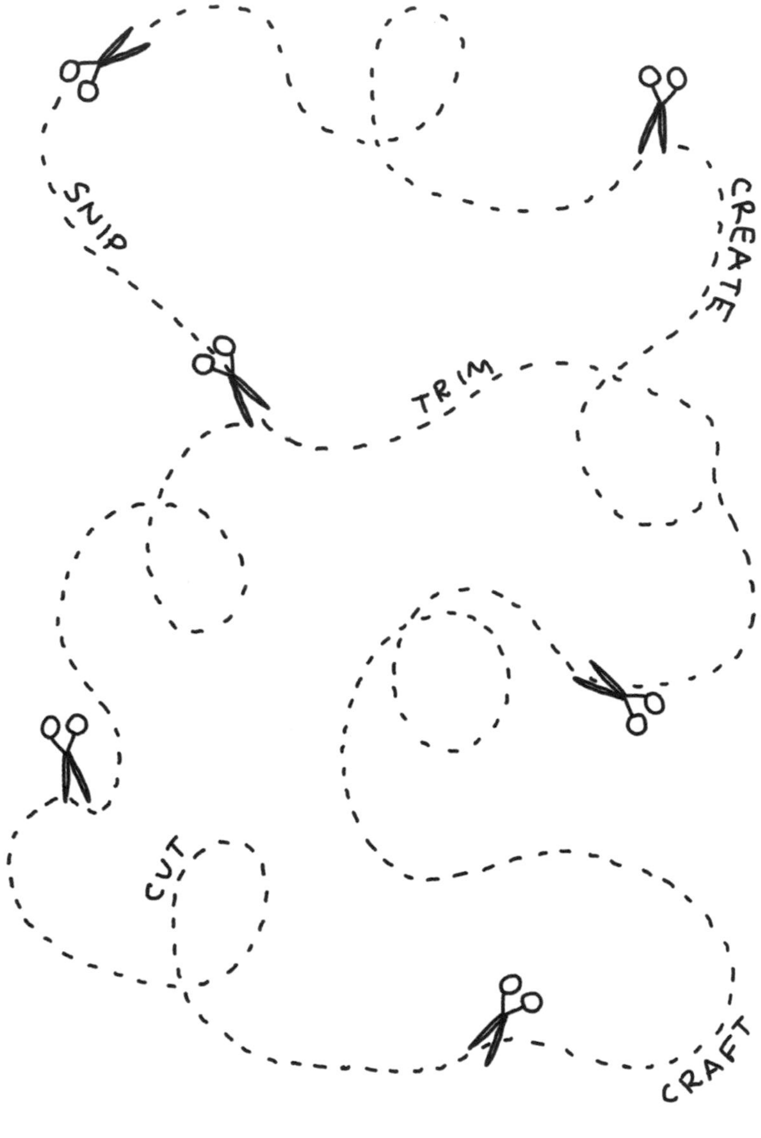
SNIP
CREATE
TRIM
CUT
CRAFT

TO ACCOMMODATE CRAFTINESS!

*Nature Walk

Take a walk outside. Bring a crayon or pencil, and make a couple of rubbings. Try a leaf, a textured rock, or tree bark!

#38

MAKE A JOKE!

LOL!

HILARIOUS!

Why did the introvert cross the road? _____

Which came first, the _____ or the _____ ?

An introvert and an extrovert walked into a bar... _____ _____ _____

You might be an introvert if: _____ _____

Knock, knock.   Who's there?

_____ ,   _____ who?

_____

#39

I live for snack time!

PASTE YOUR FAVORITE SNACK FOOD LABEL HERE!

MORE PLZ

VERY YUM

#40

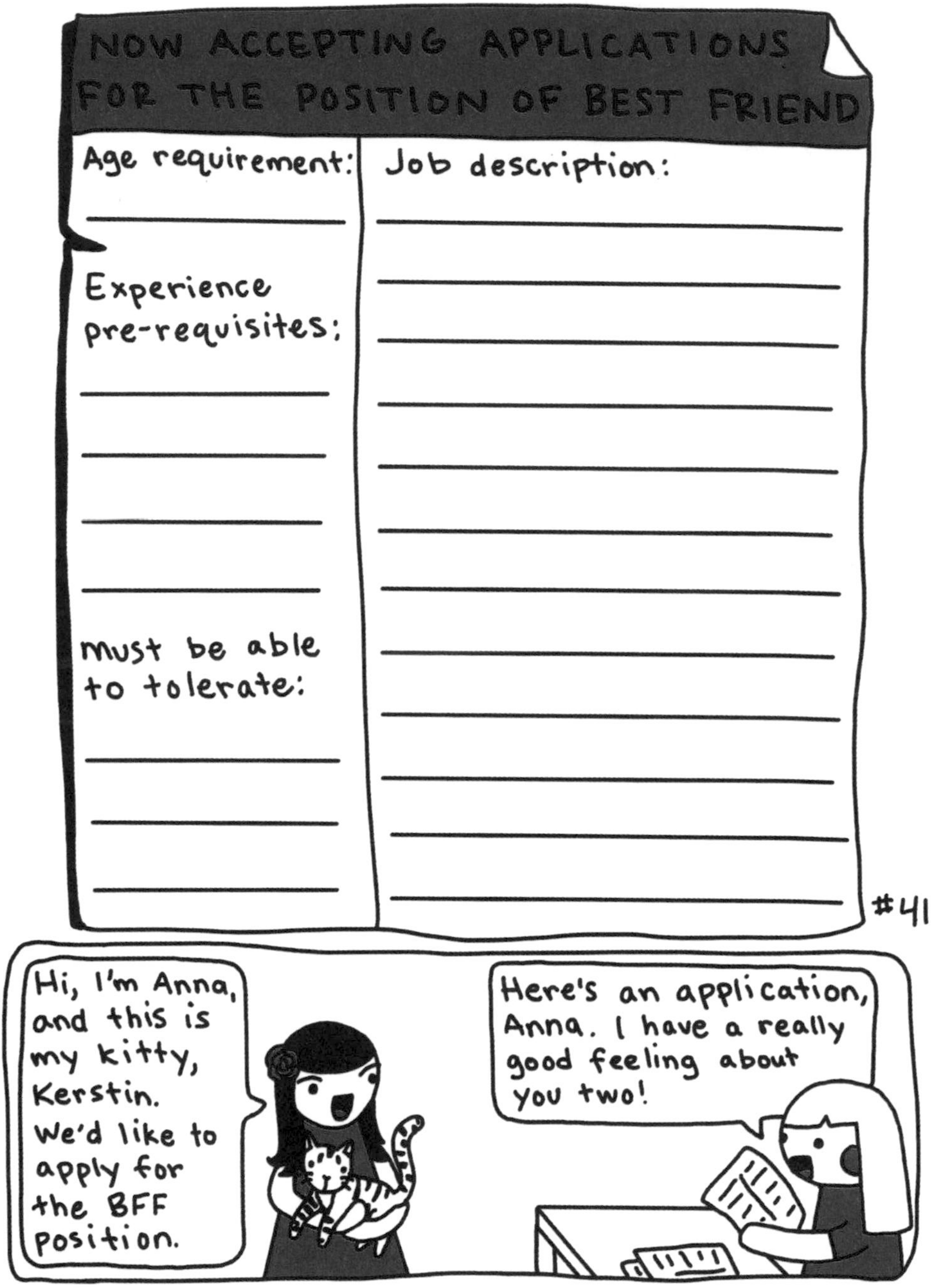
NOW ACCEPTING APPLICATIONS FOR THE POSITION OF BEST FRIEND
Age requirement:
Experience pre-requisites:
must be able to tolerate:
Job description:
#41
Hi, I'm Anna, and this is my kitty, Kerstin. We'd like to apply for the BFF position.
Here's an application, Anna. I have a really good feeling about you two!

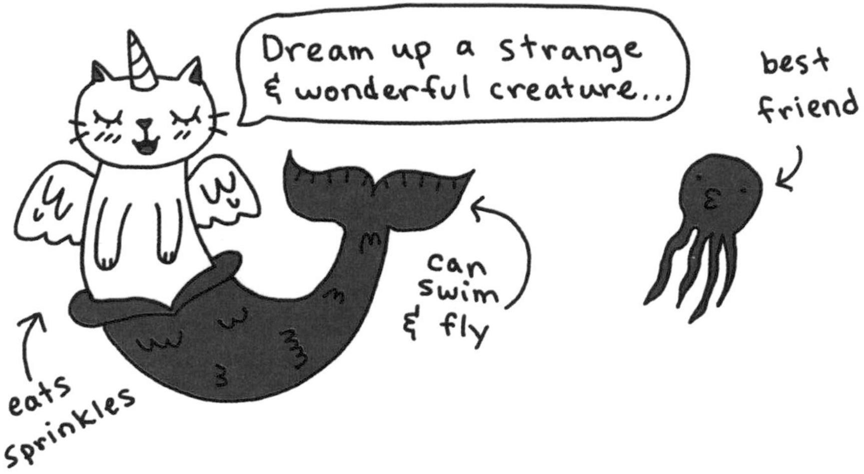
Dream up a strange & wonderful creature...
best friend
can swim & fly
eats sprinkles

#42

when I was 15, my boyfriend called & dumped me.
I handled it with grace & dignity...
Until I said, "Love you, bye!" out of habit.
Please tell me I'm not the only one...

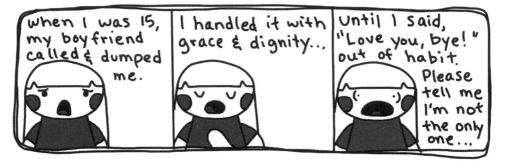

AN EMBARRASSING THING I WILL THINK ABOUT UNTIL I DIE:

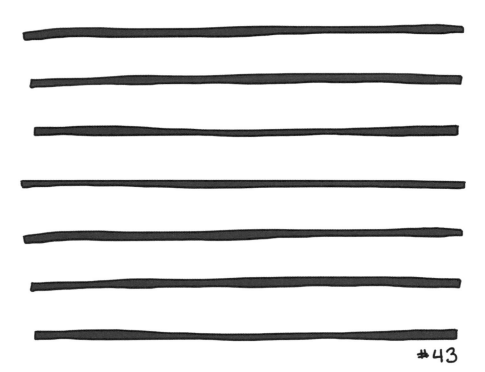

I DARE YOU

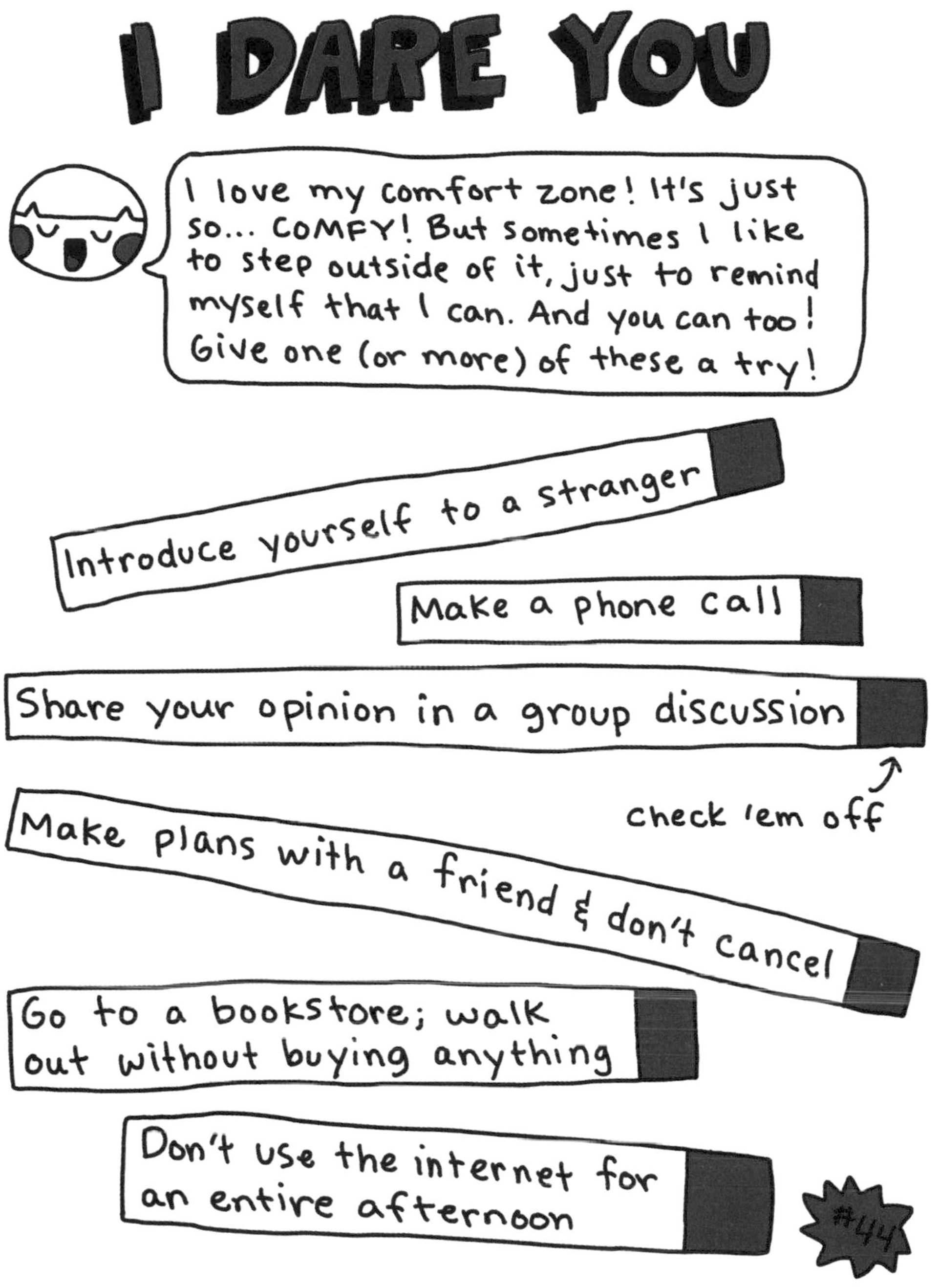

I love my comfort zone! It's just so… COMFY! But sometimes I like to step outside of it, just to remind myself that I can. And you can too! Give one (or more) of these a try!

- [ ] Introduce yourself to a stranger
- [ ] Make a phone call
- [ ] Share your opinion in a group discussion

check 'em off

- [ ] Make plans with a friend & don't cancel
- [ ] Go to a bookstore; walk out without buying anything
- [ ] Don't use the internet for an entire afternoon

#44

CUTEST DOG BREEDS

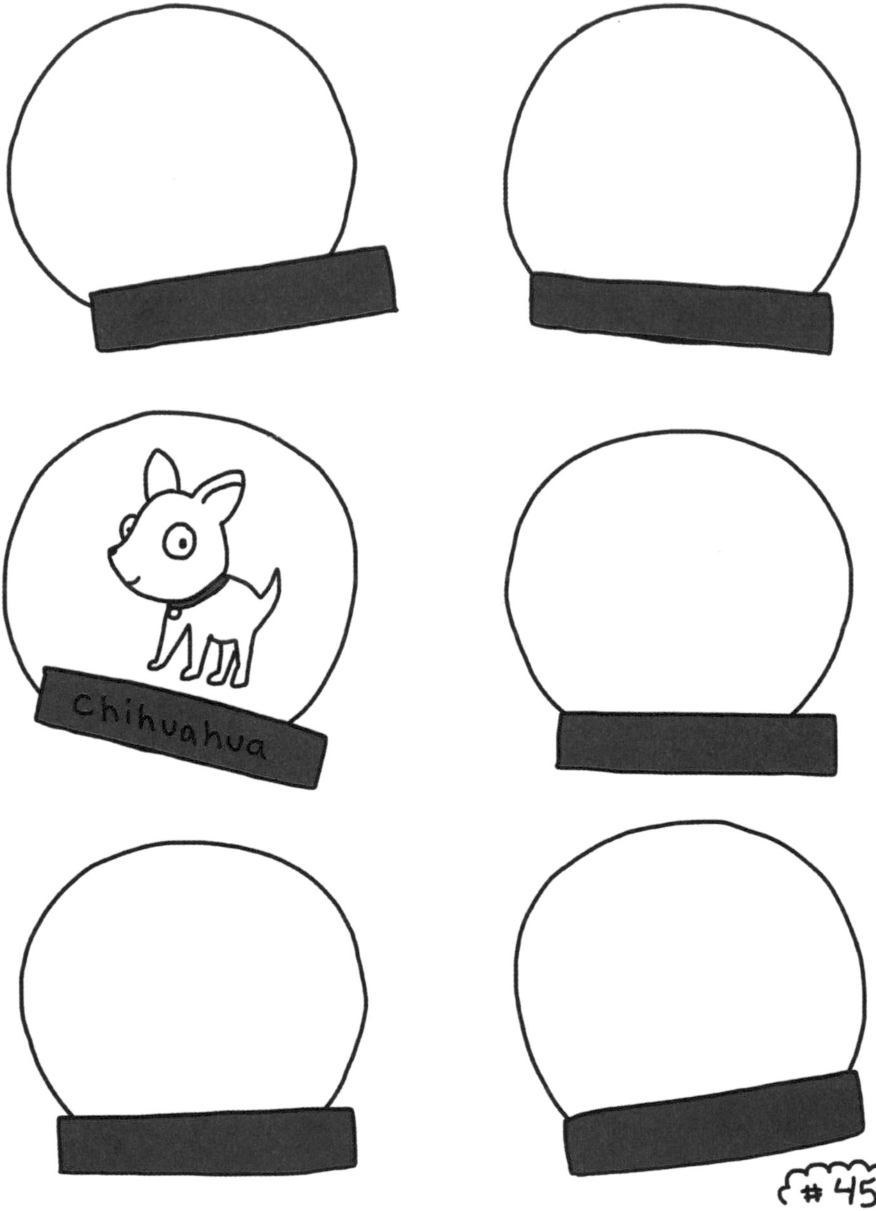
Chihuahua

MY DARKEST SECRET...

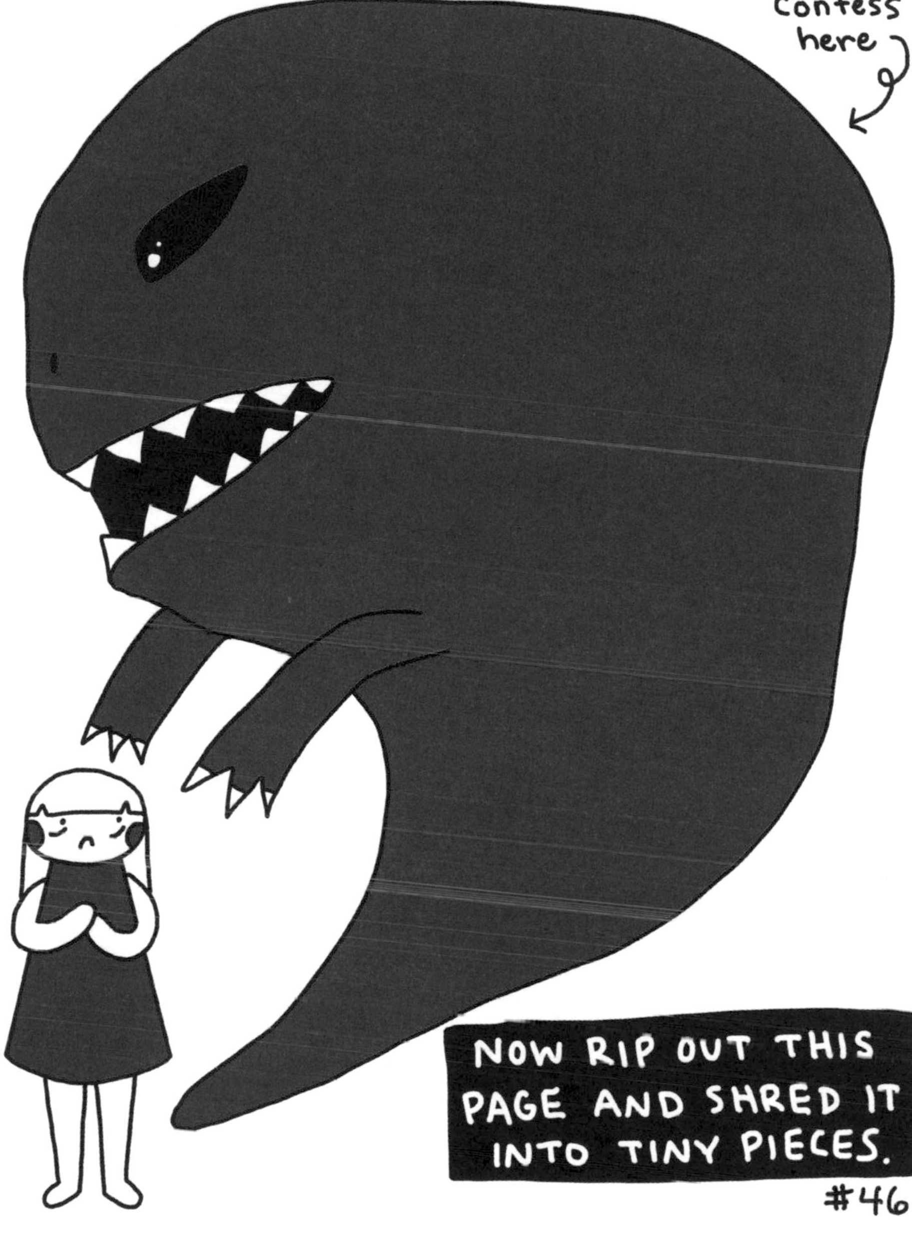
confess here
NOW RIP OUT THIS PAGE AND SHRED IT INTO TINY PIECES.

#46

THIS PAGE WILL BE DESTROYED WHEN YOU COMPLETE THE PREVIOUS ACTIVITY.

HERE
LIES
PAGE
RIPPED FROM
US TOO SOON

R.I.P, PAGE.

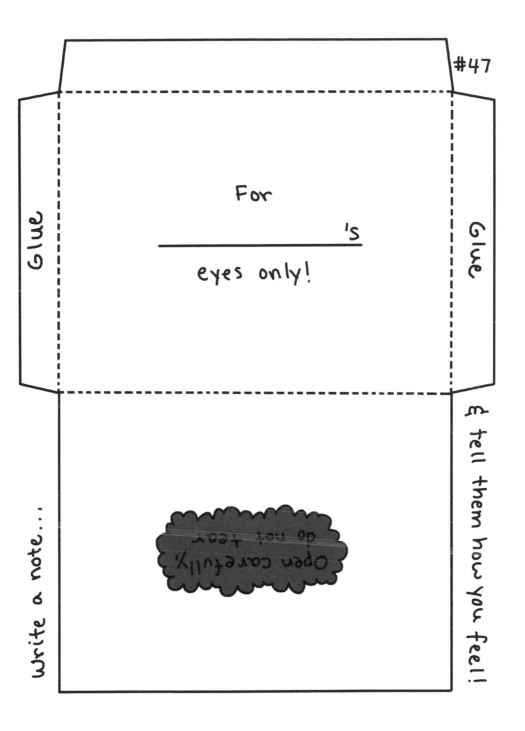

#47

Glue

Glue

For

_____'s

eyes only!

Write a note...

& tell them how you feel!

Open carefully, do not tear!

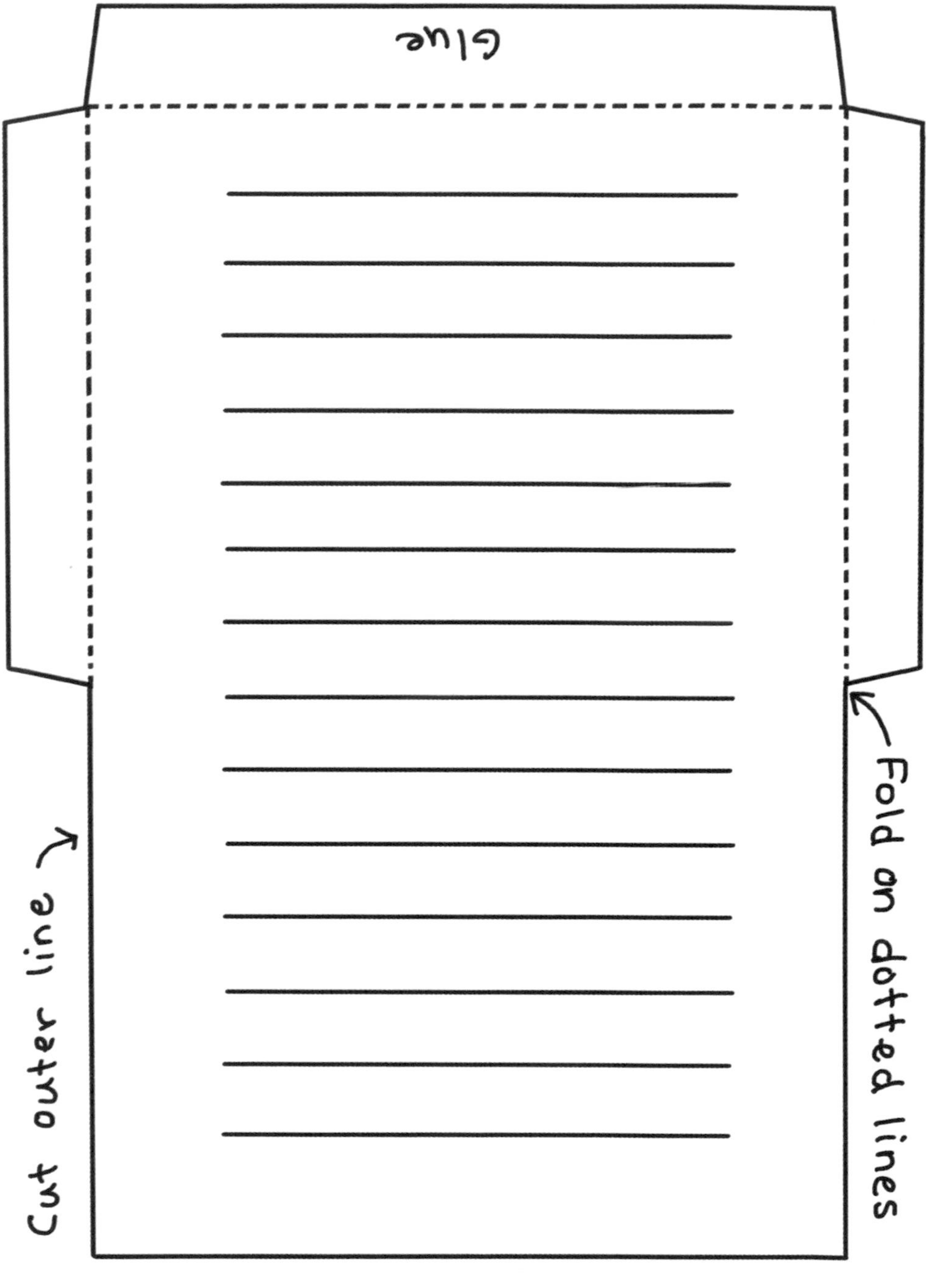
Glue
Cut outer line
Fold on dotted lines

INTROVERT MAD LIBS

Fill in the chart below, then fill in the corresponding blanks in the following story.

① Friend's name

_____

② Book title

_____

③ Color

_____

④ Item of clothing

_____

⑤ Adjective

_____

⑥ Transportation type

_____

⑦ Restaurant

_____

⑧ Texture

_____

⑨ Your grandma's name

_____

⑩ music genre

_____

⑪ Emotion

_____

⑫ Food topping

_____

⑬ Pop culture character

_____

⑭ Name of song

_____

⑮ Dance move

_____

⑯ Gymnastics move

_____

⑰ Animal

_____

#48

"You never want to go out," complained ________ [1].
"True," I admitted.
"Well, tonight, you're coming!" I sighed and put down ________ [2]. I wasn't sure what to wear, so I just put on a ________ [3] ________ [4].
"How does this look?" I asked.
"________ [5]. Now come on, let's go!"

We took a ________ [6] downtown. I hoped we were going to ________ [7], but instead we ended up at a club called ________ [8] ________ [9]. ________ [10] music filled the night air, and I felt a little ________ [11]. I noticed a hot dog cart across the street, and figured the night wouldn't be a total loss if I at least got a chili dog with ________ [12]. I ordered two, but my friend didn't want one. Actually they seemed a little embarrassed that I was eating a chili dog in line. 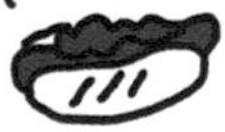

When we reached the door, the bouncer took one look at my ________ [13] backpack and refused to let us enter.

I winked at my friend. "No worries, I've got this." I slipped the bouncer my remaining chili dog. He shrugged and let us in.

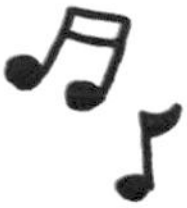

"Come on, let's dance," said my friend, dragging me onto the dance floor. ____________ (14) was playing, and I shyly began my signature move, the ____________ (15). I started to get in my groove, and noticed a crowd was gathering around me. They LOVED me! Who knew this introvert had such hidden talent?!

I attempted a ____________ (16) and, okay, it didn't go as planned, but the crowd was still smiling and taking video clips with their phones. Maybe I'd become a wealthy internet sensation & retire on a private island full of ____________ (17)s!

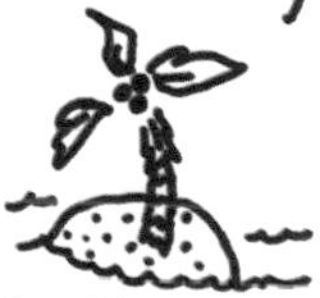

Just then, my friend yanked me off the dance floor. "What are you DOING?" I protested. "I had sick moves!"

"You looked sick all right," they agreed, pointing to a large chili smear on my butt.

I knew I should have stayed home.

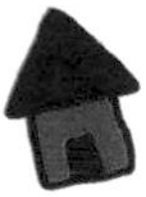

SEMI-SCIENTIFIC DIAGRAM OF

MY BRAIN

COLOR & LABEL

#49

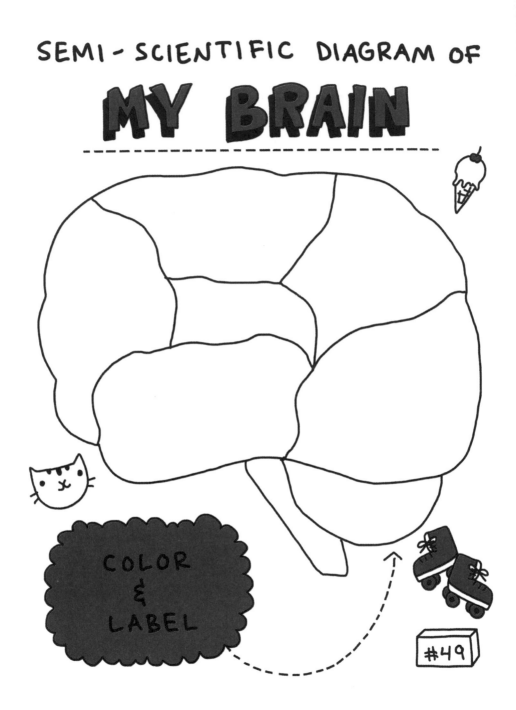

FAMILY REUNION

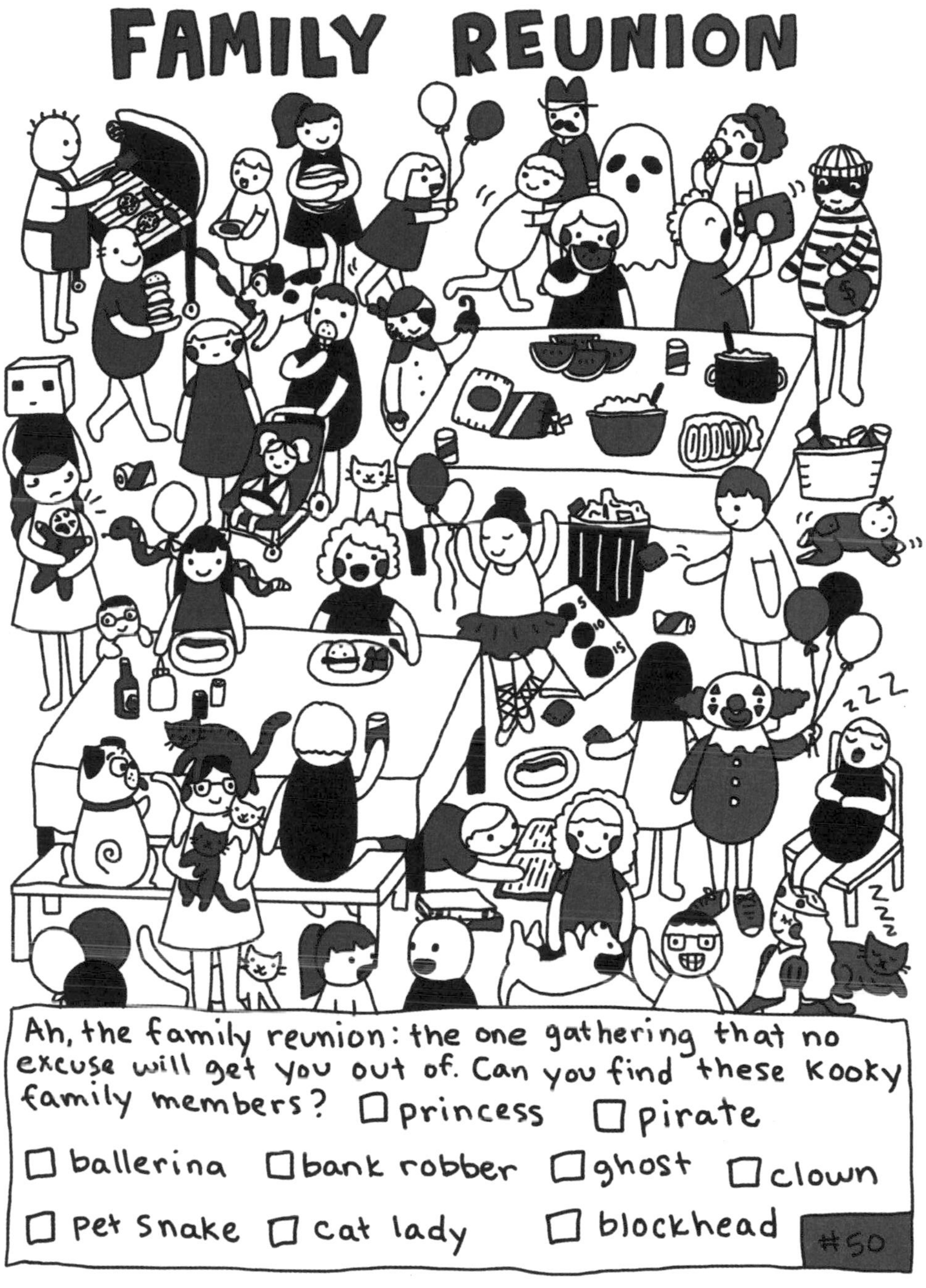

5
10
15
ZZZ
ZZZ

Ah, the family reunion: the one gathering that no excuse will get you out of. Can you find these kooky family members? ☐ princess ☐ pirate

☐ ballerina ☐ bank robber ☐ ghost ☐ clown

☐ pet snake ☐ cat lady ☐ blockhead

#50

HOW I SPEND MY TIME

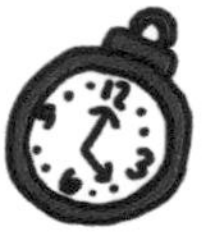

Color the slices & label the coordinating squares.

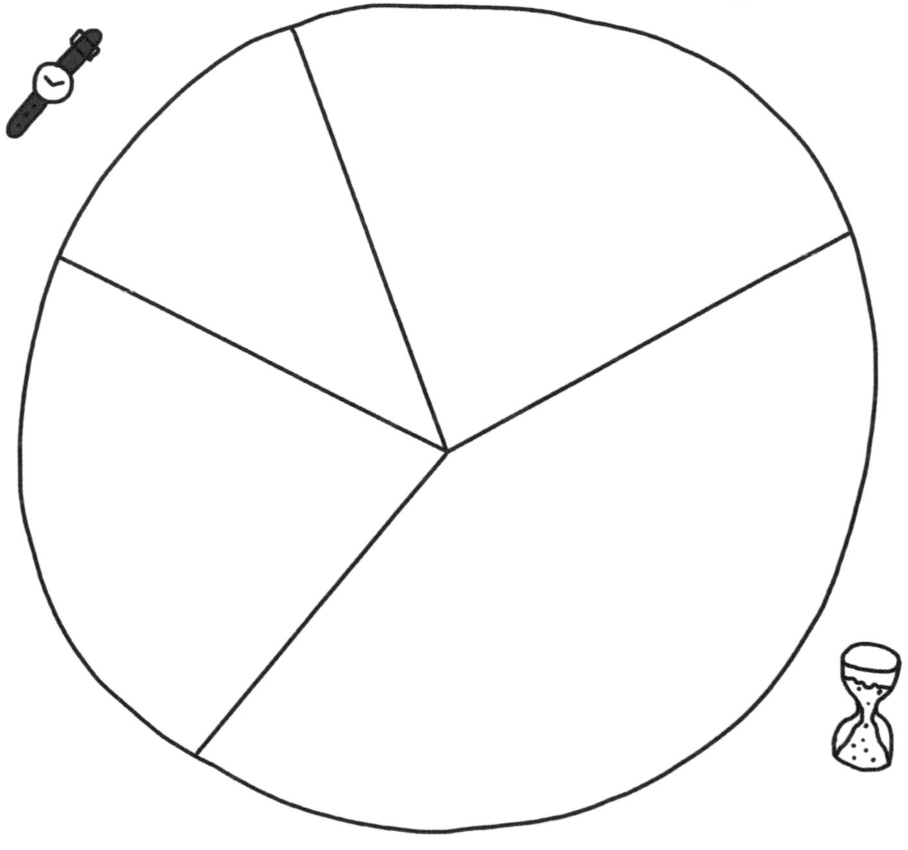

#51

ENJOY THIS PICTURE OF *Snow*!

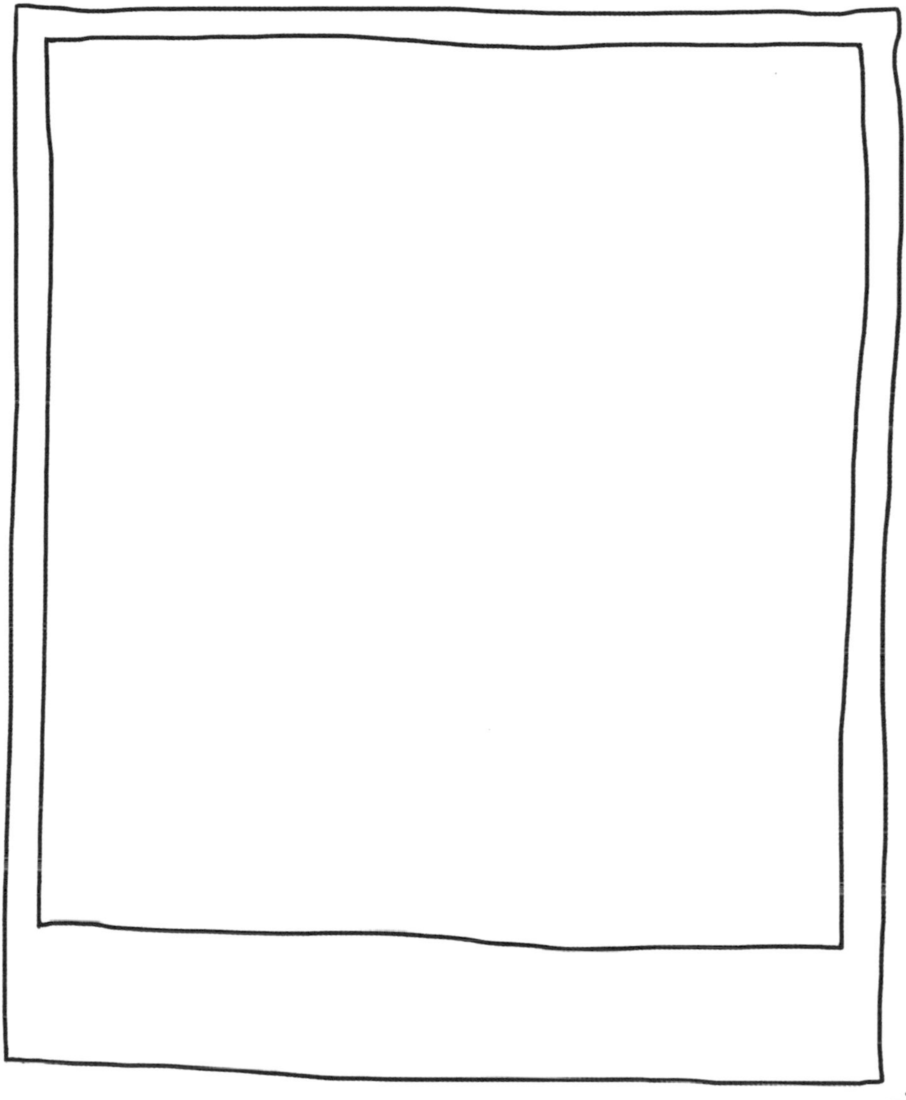

(JK, THIS PAGE IS GONNA BE CUT UP)

TRASH -OR- treasure

Cut out the words below & sort on the next page

SNAKES

MUSICALS

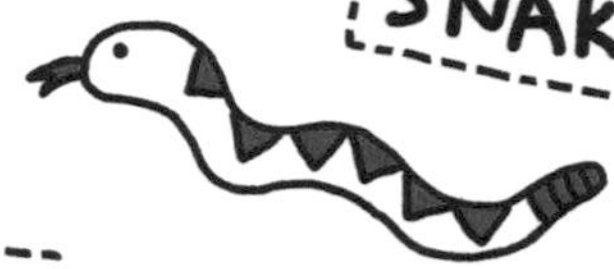

SCI-FI

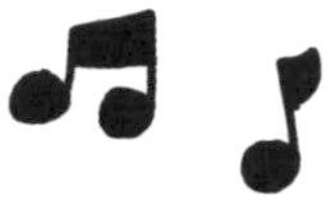

BOARD GAMES

PARTIES

HUGS

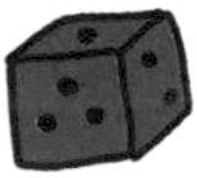

MATH

ANIME

CONCERTS

ROLLER COASTERS

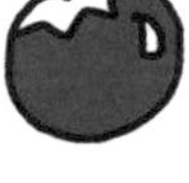

COOKING

TOMATOES

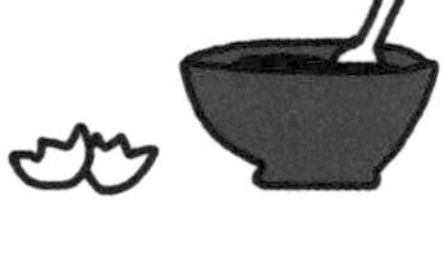

PUNS

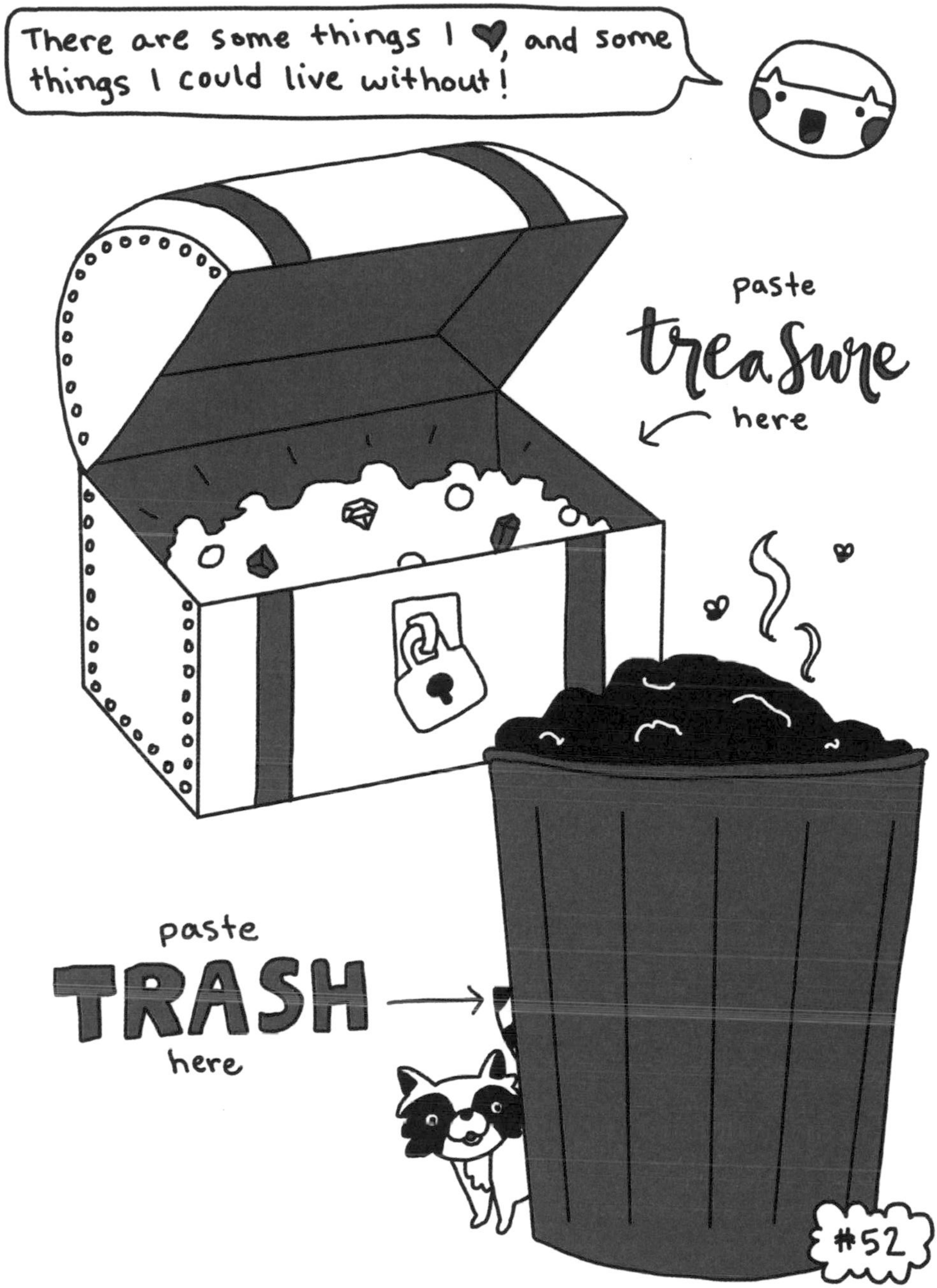
There are some things I ♥, and some things I could live without!
paste treasure here
paste TRASH here
#52

THE ULTIMATE VACATION QUIZ

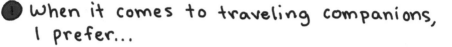

Circle your answers below to reveal your ideal vacation destination!

1 When it comes to traveling companions, I prefer...

A) To go solo! If it isn't a vacation from people, it isn't a vacation.

B) To have one good friend by my side. You've gotta have someone to make memories with!

C) To hang out with the locals. After all, they know the best secret spots!

2 The one thing I couldn't travel without is...

A) A new novel.

B) Practical shoes.

C) The Yelp app.

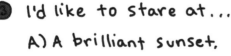

3 I'd like to stare at...

A) A brilliant sunset.

B) A night sky sprinkled with stars.

C) The alluring twinkle of city lights.

4. when it comes to food, I choose...

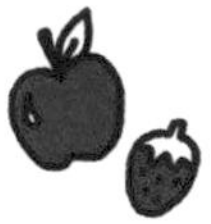

A) Organic & vegan, please. Fresh fruits & veggies for the win!

B) Simple home cooking. Tried & true comfort food for me!

C) Something exotic. New dishes add spice to life!

5. I long for...

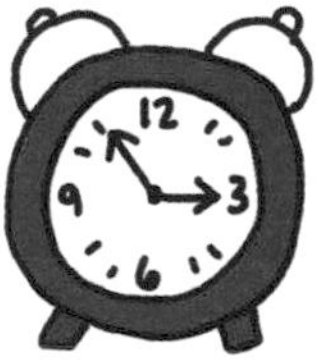

12
3
6
9

A) Serenity

B) Adventure

C) Enlightenment

6. my favorite time of day is...

A) Afternoon! Perfect for basking in the sunshine.

B) Morning! Crisp, cool mornings + a mug of hot coffee = perfection.

C) Evening! Dinner & deep conversation.

7. I would rather...

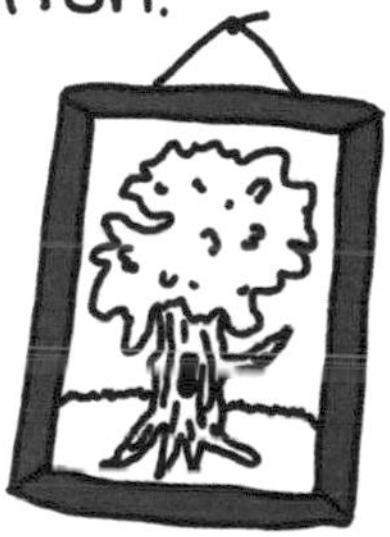

A) Nap under a tree

B) Climb a tree

C) Admire a painting of a tree

TALLY YOUR ANSWERS & TURN PAGE →

A's ____ B's ____ C's ____

Mostly A's **ISLAND RETREAT**

You need a vacation that's pure rest and relaxation! Lounge on the beach and sip from a coconut on your island retreat. Read a book beneath a palm tree and soak up the sun. Replenish with a solitary stroll along the shoreline at sunset. You were made for island living!

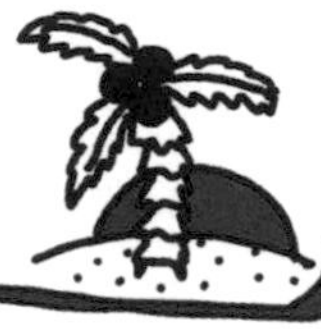

Mostly B's **MOUNTAIN ADVENTURE**

Get back to nature with a mountain adventure! Bring your best friend (or your dog!) and enjoy the peaceful seclusion of a rustic cabin. Cook over a campfire and talk under the stars. Spend your mornings exploring the woods, identifying flowers, and watching for wildlife. Feeling extra adventurous? Try rock climbing or whitewater rafting!

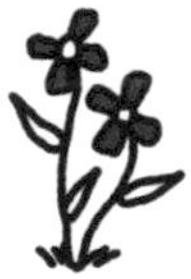

Mostly C's **EUROPEAN TOUR**

A tour of Europe will fulfill your desire for new experiences! Enjoy the rich culture as you meander through museums, investigate historical sites, and explore outdoor markets. Pop into a small cafe or restaurant and order an authentic dish. Strike up a conversation with local residents for an immersive vacation experience. Ciao and adieu, darling!

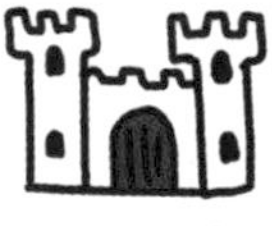

COLOR THE PHRASES YOU'VE HEARD

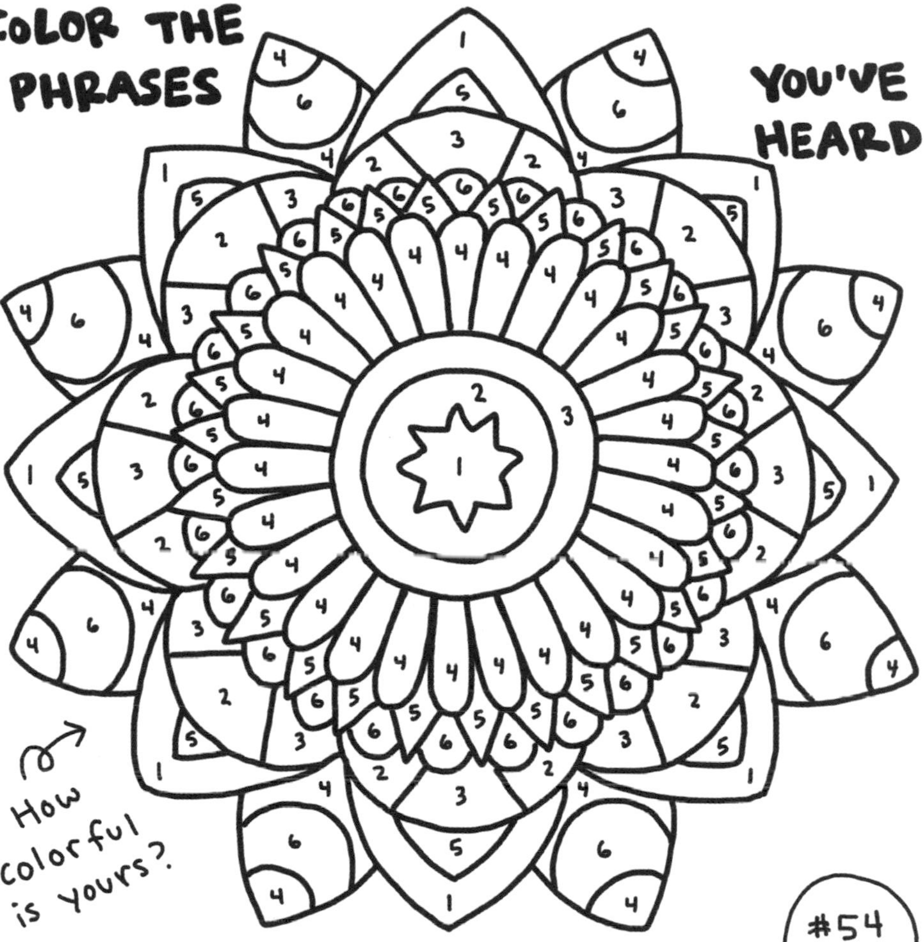

How colorful is yours?

#54

"Why are you leaving early?"
1- Royal Blue

"You're different."
2- Teal

"You're anti-social."
3- Yellow

"Are you shy?"
4- Red

"You should talk more."
5- Fuchsia Pink

"Aren't you lonely?"
6- Purple

SCRAMBLED CATS

UNSCRAMBLE THESE KITTY-THEMED WORDS!

TACINP _ _ _ _ _ _

BRHILALA _ _ _ _ _ _ _ _

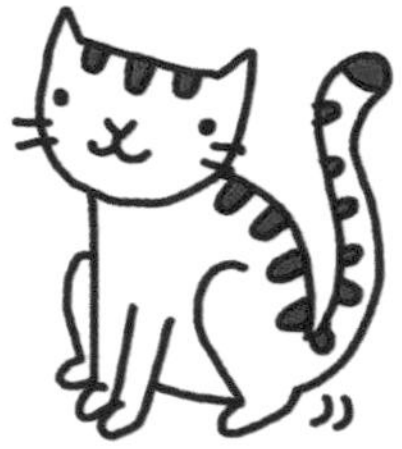
SCRITCH
SCRITCH

TIRLTE _ _ _ _ _ _

LABL FO NYRA _ _ _ _ _ _ _ _ _ _

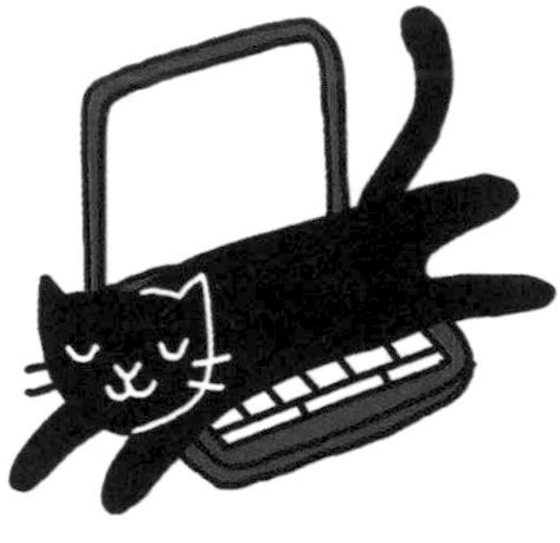

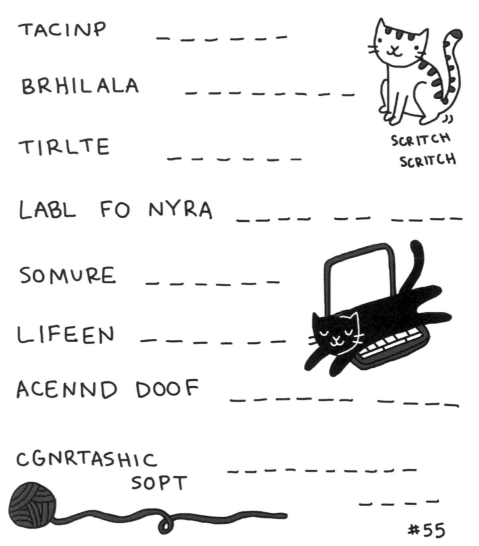

SOMURE _ _ _ _ _ _

LIFEEN _ _ _ _ _ _

ACENND DOOF _ _ _ _ _ _ _ _ _ _

CGNRTASHIC _ _ _ _ _ _ _ _ _ _

SOPT _ _ _ _

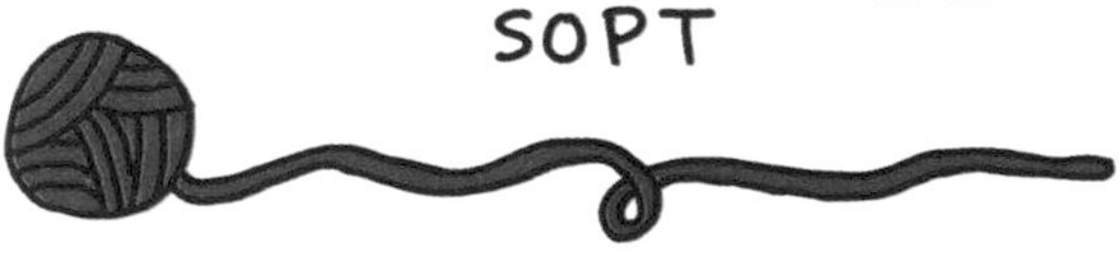

List one thing you accomplished today:

Wow, you deserve a treat! Seriously, go buy yourself a little something-something and then paste your receipt here

TREAT YO'SELF

#56

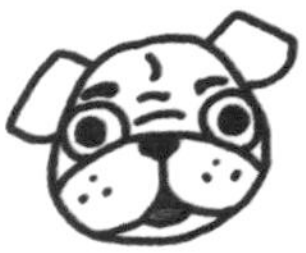

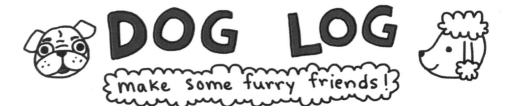

DOG LOG

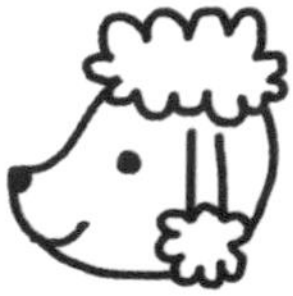

make some furry friends!

Doggo's Name	Breed	Location met

#57

WHAT'S IN MY BAG?

#58

This is a sketch of the main character in the book I'm reading. His/her name is

_____.

One thing I like about this character is how he/she _____

_____

_____.

If there was something I could change about him/her, it's...

_____

_____.

I hope this character decides to

_____

before the end of the book!

#60

MAKE A BOOKMARK

Oh!
For me?!
You shouldn't have!

Punch a hole. Tie a ribbon through it!

Cut out on solid line →

TIP

To make it extra sturdy, cover both sides with clear packing tape.

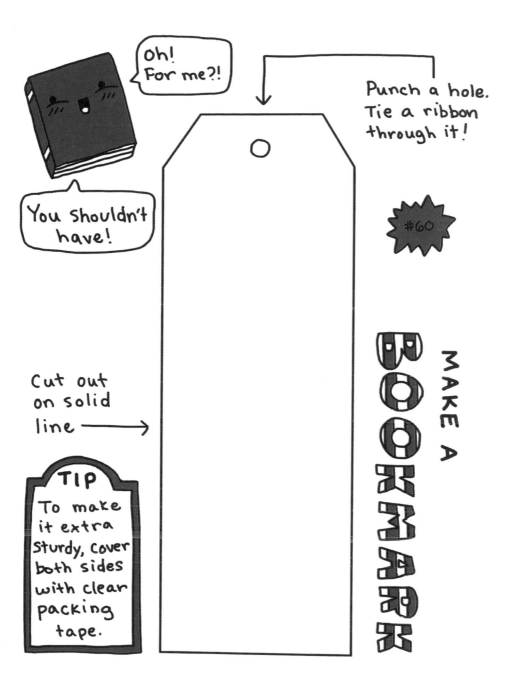

THIS
PAGE IS
BLANK
FOR A
REASON.

YOU'RE
JUST
GONNA
HAVE TO
TRUST
ME ON
THIS.

IT'S A LITTLE BIT

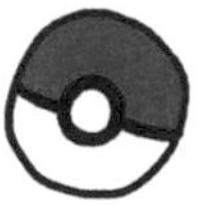

NERDY,

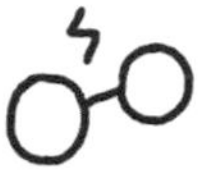

BUT I REALLY LIKE...

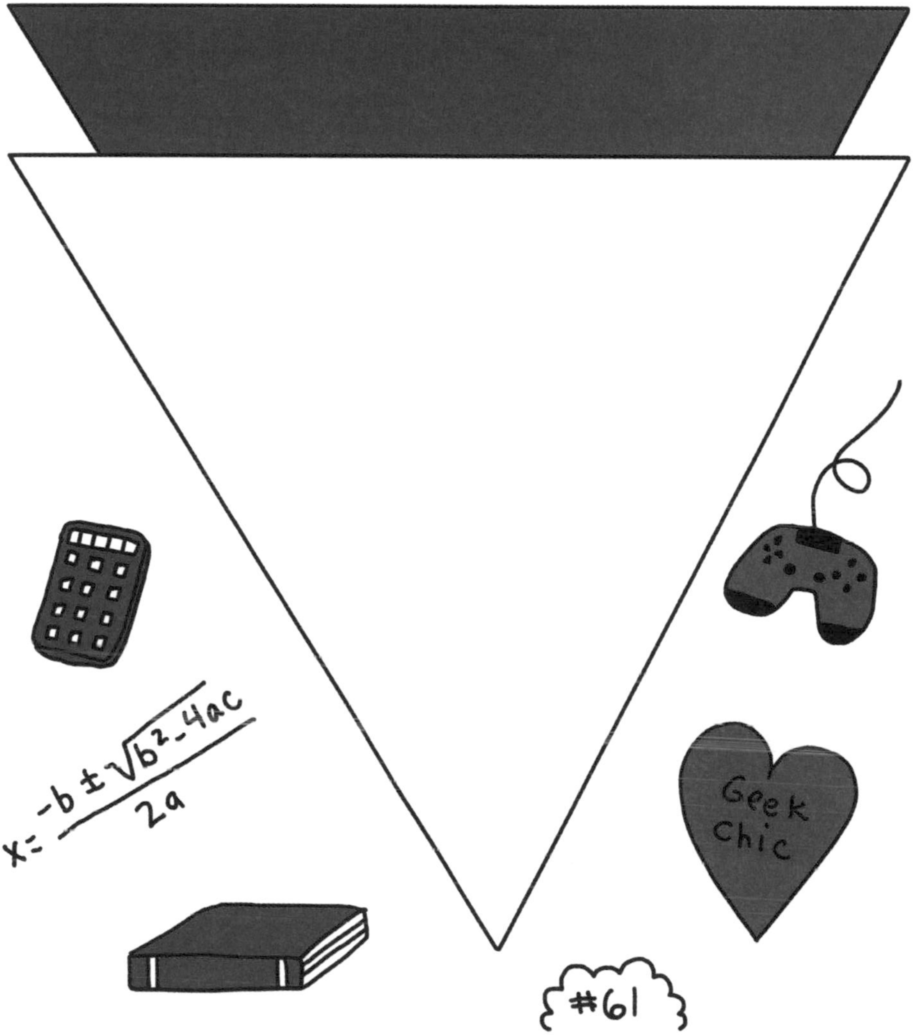

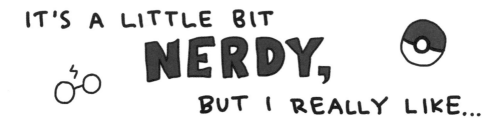

$x = \frac{-b \pm \sqrt{b^2 - 4ac}}{2a}$
Geek chic

#61

RANK THESE FROM 1-10, IN ORDER OF
AWKWARDNESS

	#
Accidentally hitting "reply all"	
Opening a gift in front of a group	
Small talk about the weather	
Forgetting someone's name	
Moist & floppy handshake	
When you're told to "find a partner"	
Waiting in line in a bathroom	
Unintentionally liking an ex's photo	
Realizing your zipper was down	
Knowing only the host at a party	

#62

Introverts are okay with being different. In fact, we take pride in being as unique as a fingerprint!

THUMBPRINT ART

#63

Color your thumb and stamp your fingerprint on the paper. Turn it into a creative creature. Repeat.

label & color these

INTROVERT AWARD RIBBONS

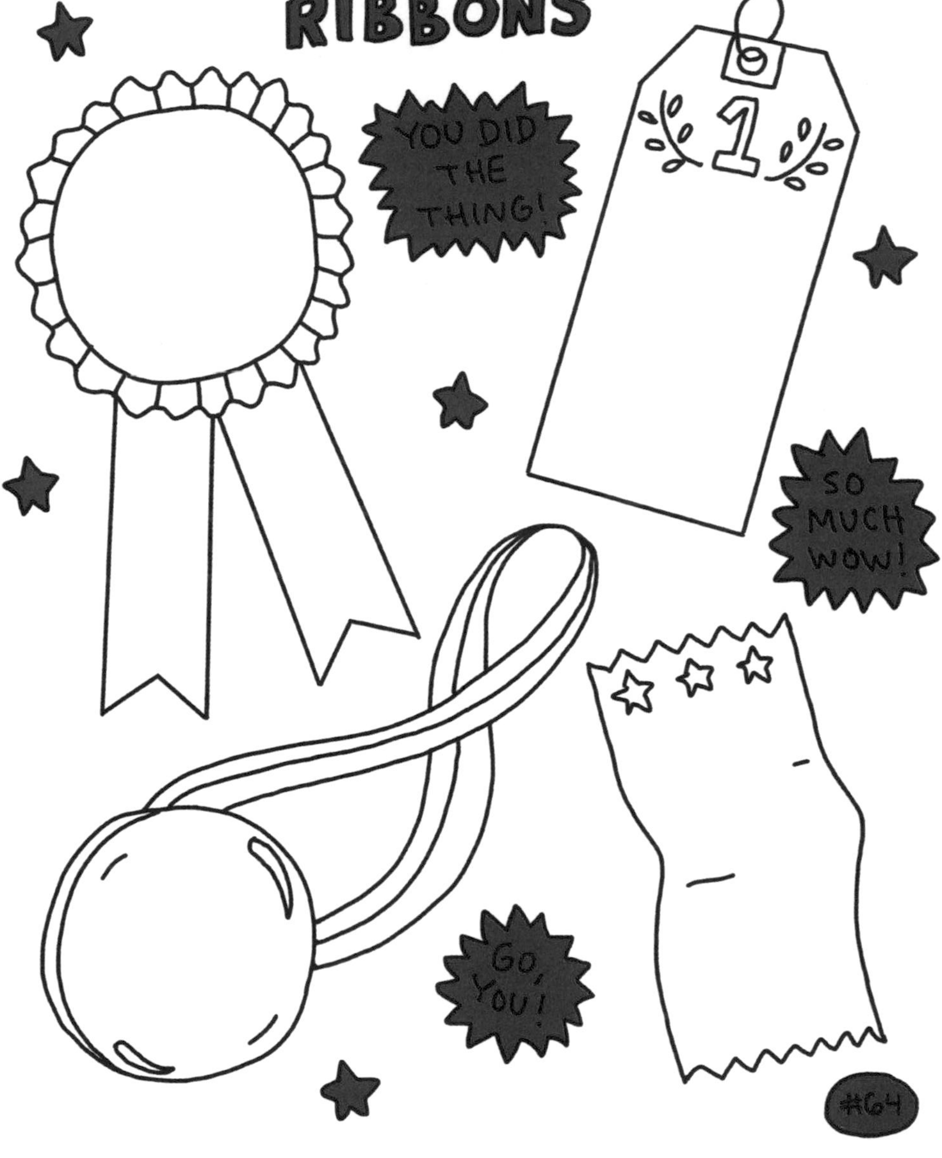
YOU DID THE THING!
SO MUCH WOW!
GO, YOU!

#64

A POEM ABOUT

Solitude

_____

_____

_____

_____

_____

_____

_____

_____

_____

_____

#65

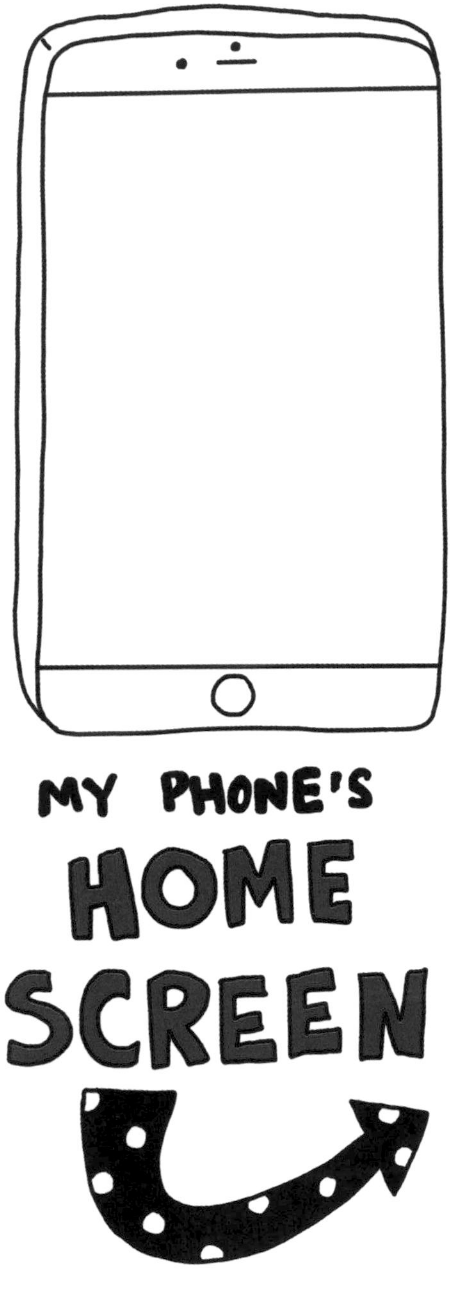

MY PHONE'S
LOCK SCREEN

MY PHONE'S
HOME SCREEN

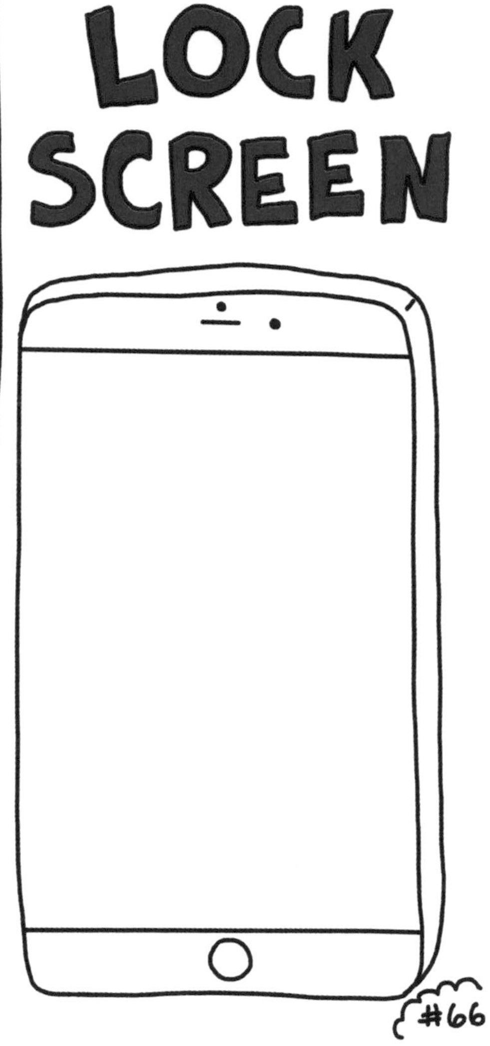

#66

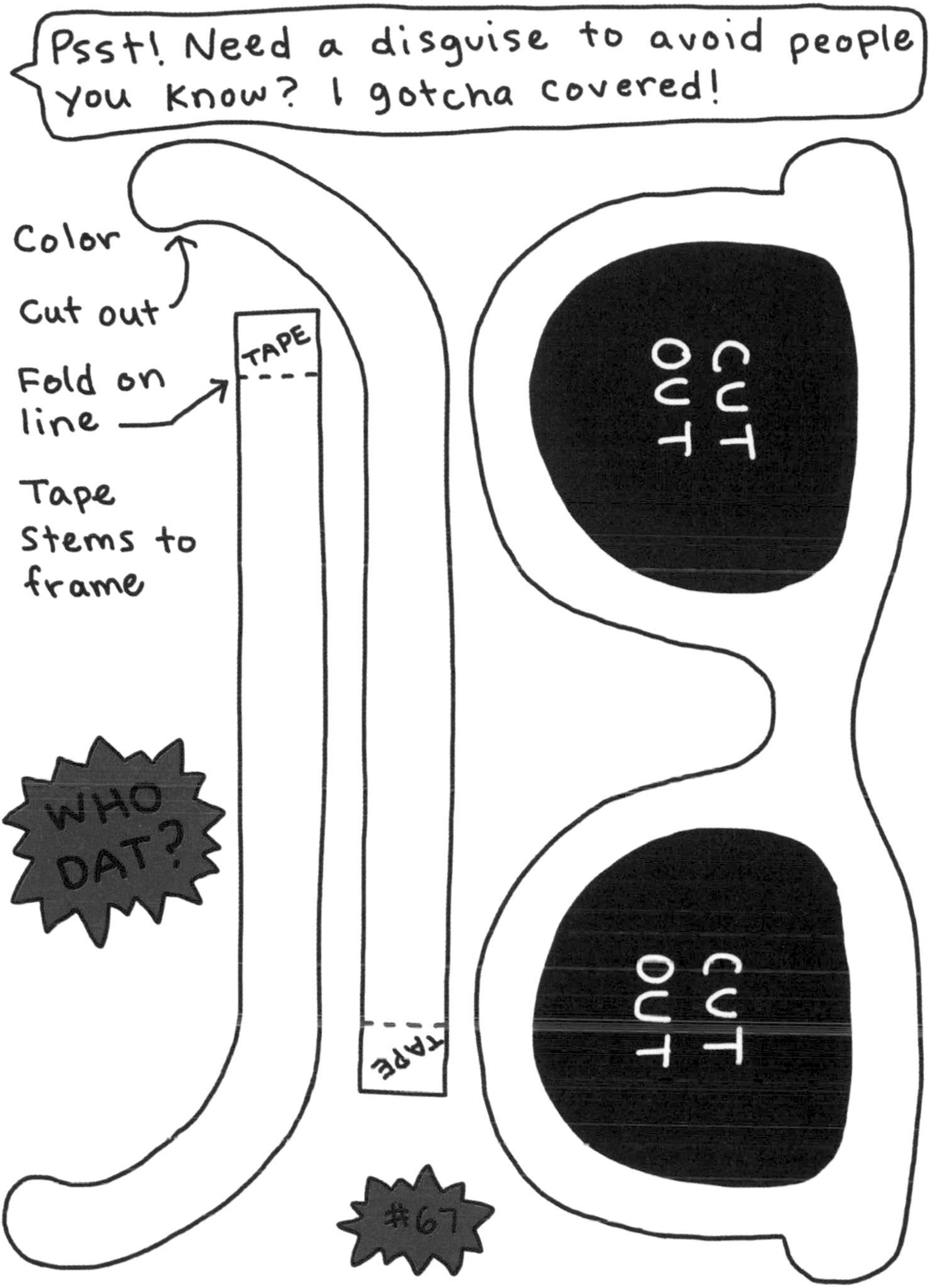
Psst! Need a disguise to avoid people you know? I gotcha covered!
Color
Cut out
Fold on line
Tape stems to frame
TAPE
TAPE
CUT OUT
CUT OUT
WHO DAT?
#67

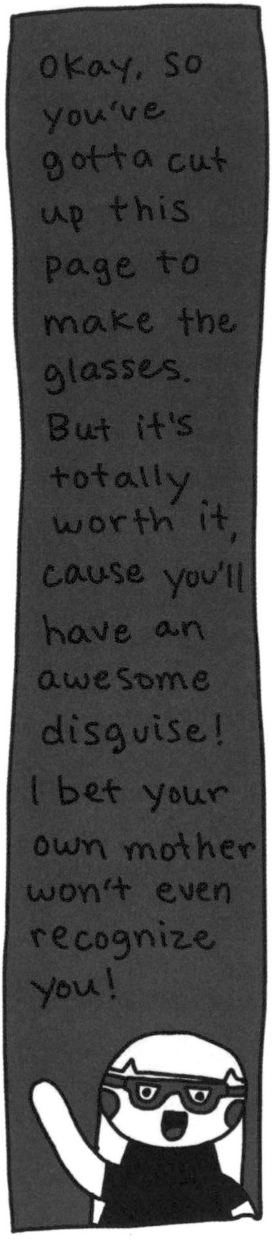
Okay, so you've gotta cut up this page to make the glasses. But it's totally worth it, cause you'll have an awesome disguise! I bet your own mother won't even recognize you!

my LIFE GOALS
(some serious, some not-so-serious)

Learn to flambé

mac &
cheese

then flambé all
the things!

_____

_____

_____

_____

_____

_____

_____

_____

_____

_____

_____

_____

_____

#68

FORTUNE TELLER INSTRUCTIONS

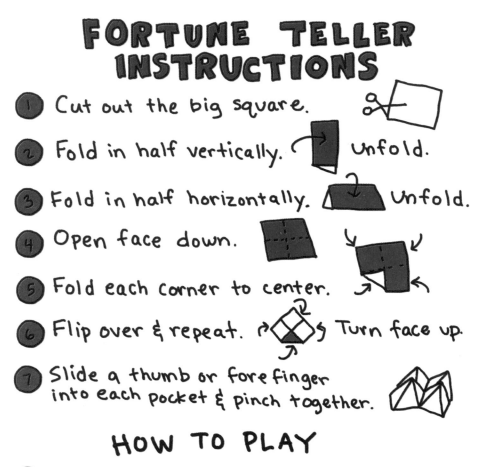

1. Cut out the big square. 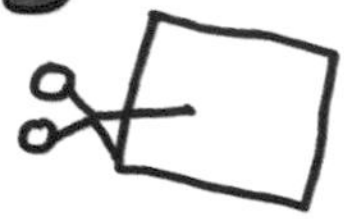
2. Fold in half vertically. 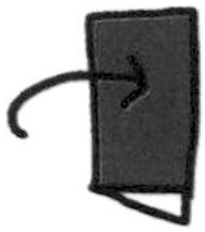 Unfold.
3. Fold in half horizontally. 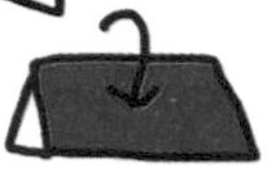 Unfold.
4. Open face down. 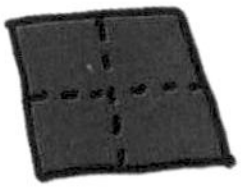
5. Fold each corner to center. 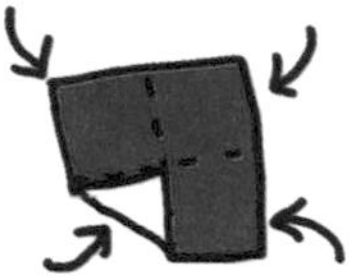
6. Flip over & repeat. 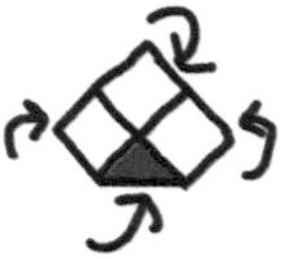 Turn face up.
7. Slide a thumb or fore finger into each pocket & pinch together. 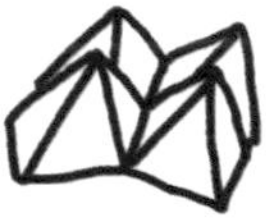

HOW TO PLAY

A. Choose a food pic. Spell the name of it out loud, pinching or pulling the corners together once for each letter.
B. Pick a number that's visible. Count to that # while pinching/pulling.
C. Choose a number & open it to reveal your fortune!

#69

INTROVERT FORTUNE TELLER

mystical!

magical!

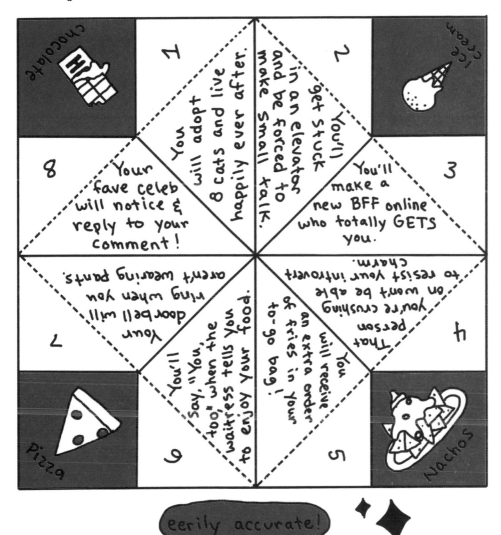

chocolate

ice cream

1

2

You'll adopt 8 cats and live happily ever after.

You'll get stuck in an elevator and be forced to make small talk.

8

3

Your fave celeb will notice & reply to your comment!

You'll make a new BFF online who totally GETS you.

7

4

Your doorbell will ring when you aren't wearing pants.

That person you're crushing on won't be able to resist your introvert charm.

Pizza

Nachos

6

5

You'll say "You, too!" when the waitress tells you to enjoy your food.

You will receive an extra order of fries in your to-go bag!

eerily accurate!

THIS PAGE MUST BE SACRIFICED FOR YOUR FORTUNE TELLER.

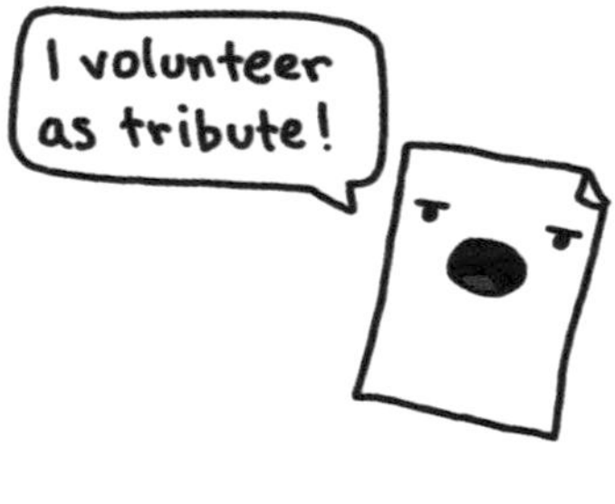
I volunteer as tribute!

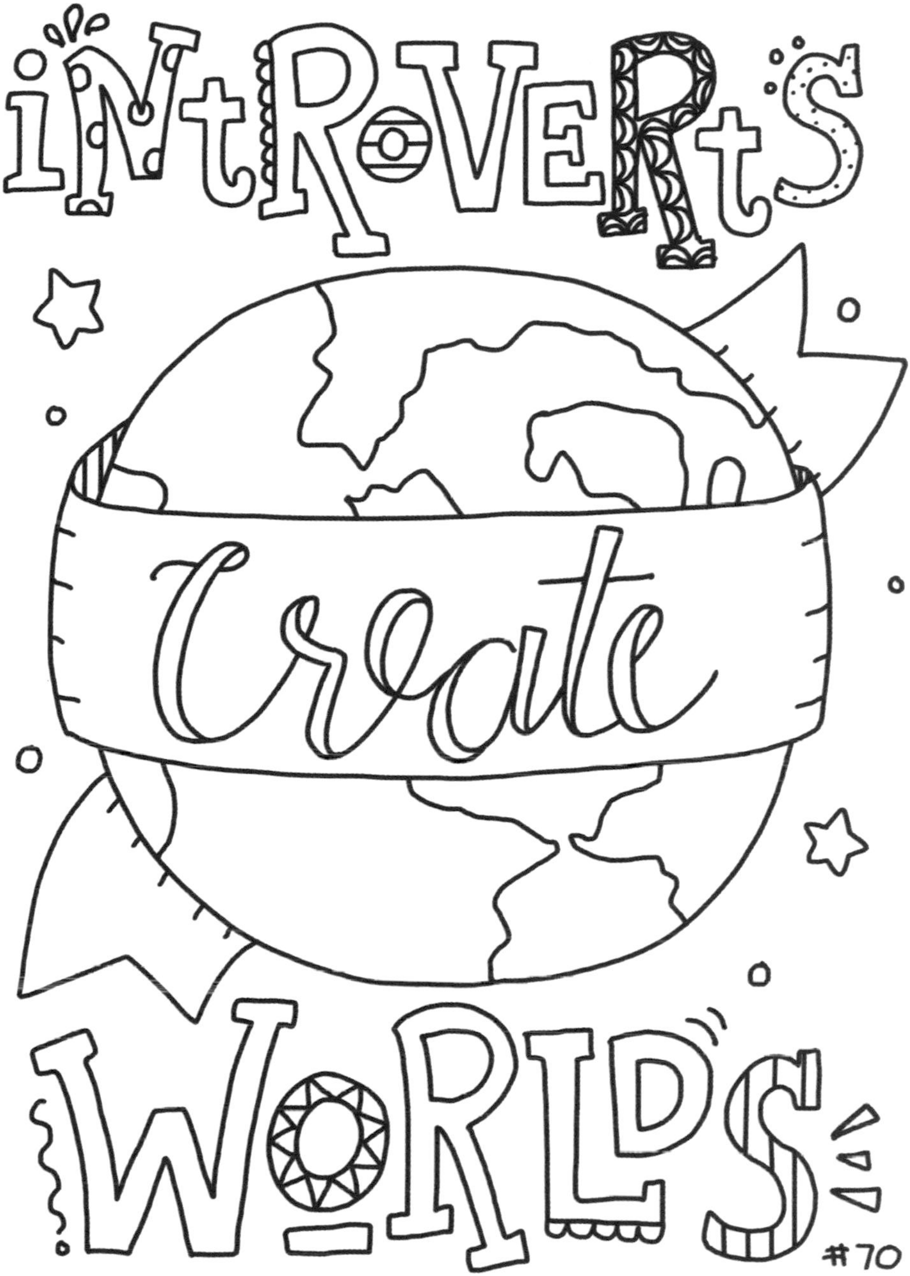
Introverts
Create
Worlds

#70

AWKWARD

STUFF I'VE SAID

OMG

WHY

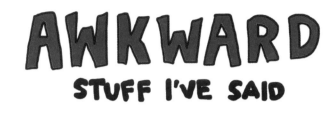

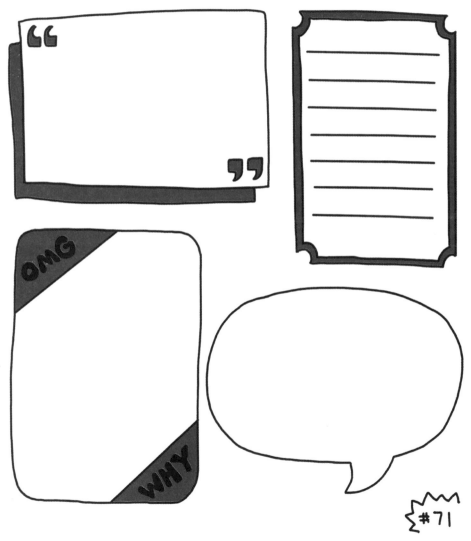

#71

TOTALLY ANNOYING THINGS

when you're wearing headphones & people talk to you anyways

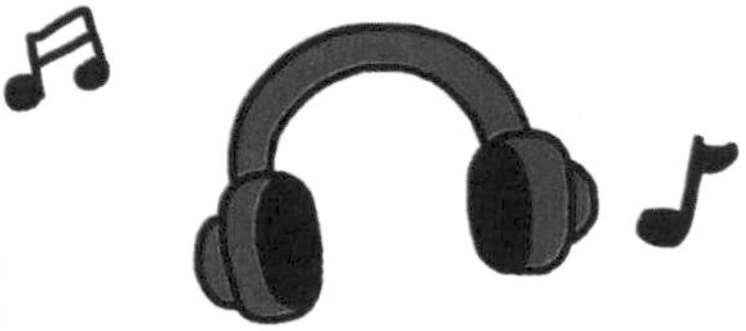

When someone calls instead of texting

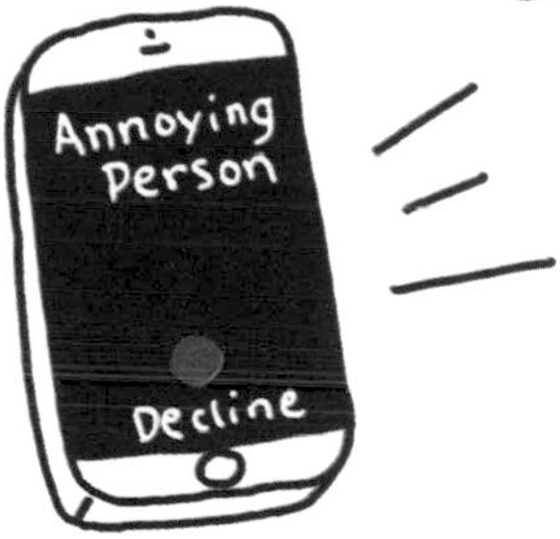
Annoying Person
Decline

when Redbox doesn't have the movie you want, so you settle for something terrible

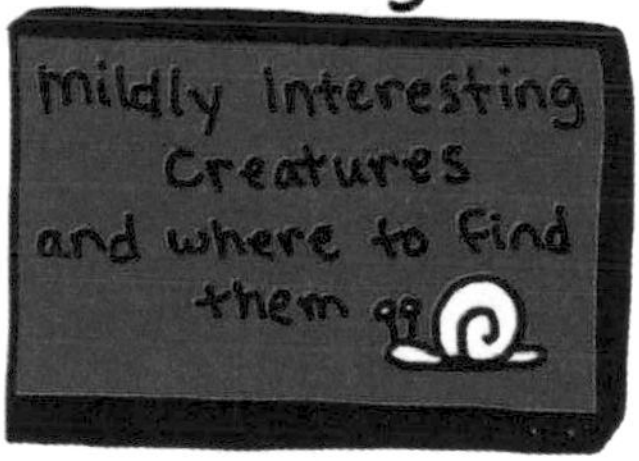
mildly interesting Creatures and where to find them

#72

MY PERFECT EVENING
WOULD INCLUDE...

☐ _____

☐ _____

☐ _____

☐ _____

☐ _____

☐ _____

☐ _____

☐ _____

nobody else

blanket cocoon

pizza

#73

Love It -OR- HATE IT?

SCENT EDITION

COLOR THE ♡ OR THE 💔

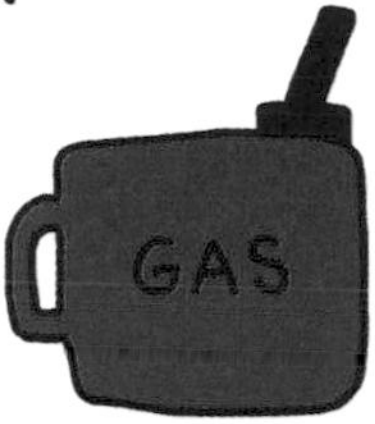
GAS

Gasoline

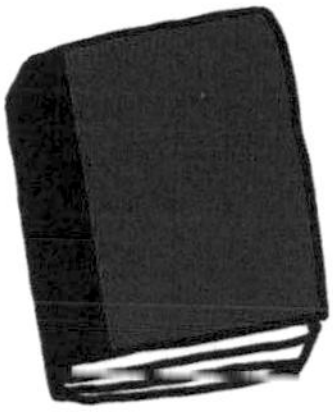

Book pages

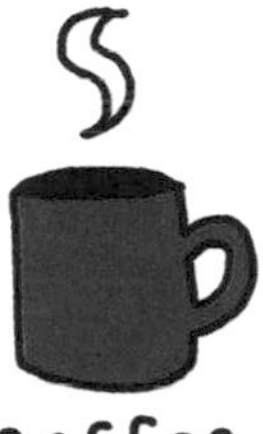

coffee

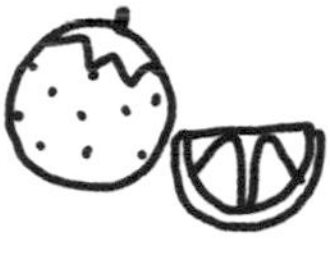

oranges

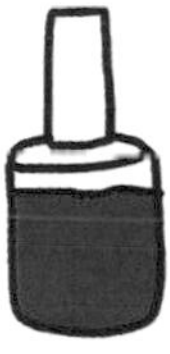

nail polish

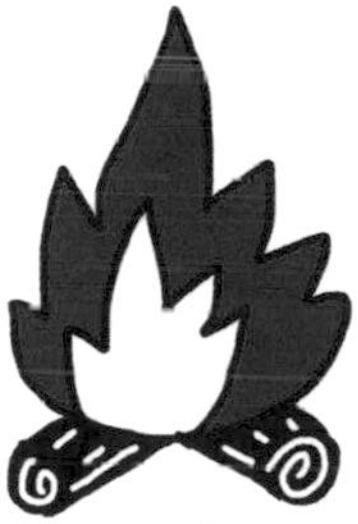

campfire

#74

OFFICIAL FOOD DARE RECORD

Red Ingredient	White Ingredient	Rating
+		☆☆☆☆☆
+		☆☆☆☆☆
+		☆☆☆☆☆
+		☆☆☆☆☆

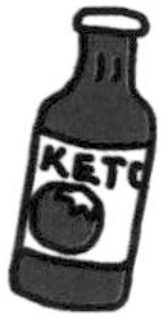

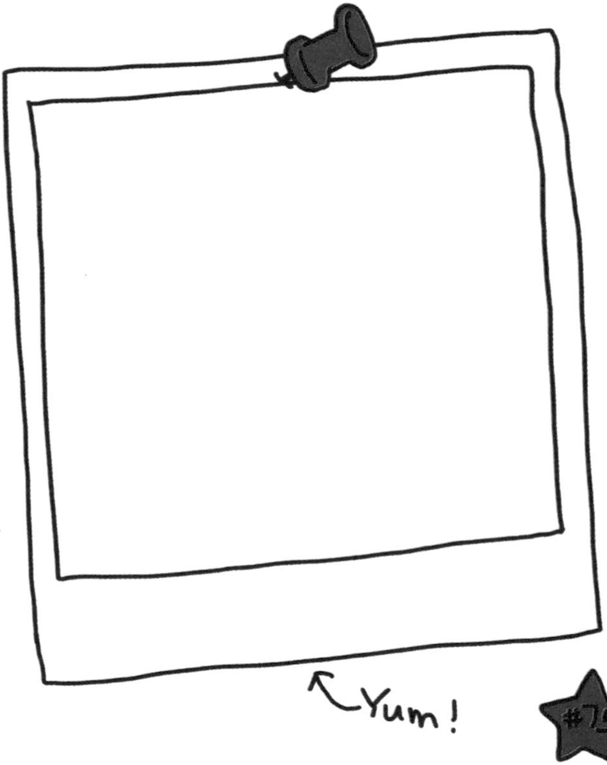

A picture of my fave food dare concoction

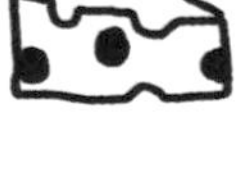

Yum!

INSTRUCTIONS

Cut out the strips & make a separate pile for red & white. Choose one strip from each pile without looking. Try the combo* & record your findings on the opposite page! ----

<--

Potato chips	yogurt
apple -or- banana	Ketchup
tortilla	peanut butter
carrot -or- celery	maple syrup
cereal	cheese
lunch meat	Salad dressing
cracker	honey
lettuce	soy sauce -or- hot sauce
ice cream	butter
pickle	salsa
popcorn	jelly

*allergic? Swap in your own ideas!

BLANK PAGE HAIKU

Embrace the blank page.
The absence of things brings peace.
Breathe in emptiness.

This page left blank for meditative purposes.
(Also, it's gonna get ripped out.)

SORT YOUR FAMILY & FRIENDS!

INTROVERT *OR* EXTROVERT

#76

DOODLE THE
PERFECT PIZZA

sooo good!
nom nom

Ordered from:

Crust type:

Toppings:

#77

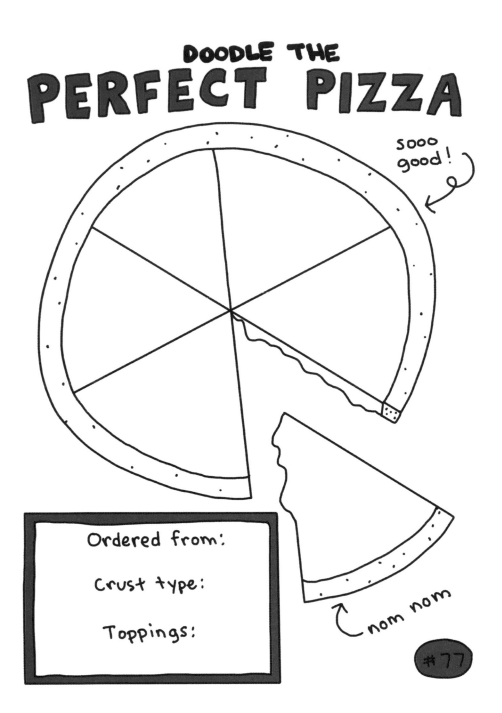

SONGS THAT SPEAK TO MY SOUL

Song: _____

Artist: _____

Lovable lyrics: _____

_____

_____

_____

Song: _____

Artist: _____

Lovable lyrics: _____

_____

_____

_____

Song: _____

Artist: _____

Lovable lyrics: _____

_____

_____

_____

Song: _____

Artist: _____

Lovable lyrics: _____

_____

_____

_____

#78

EXCELLENT EXCUSES

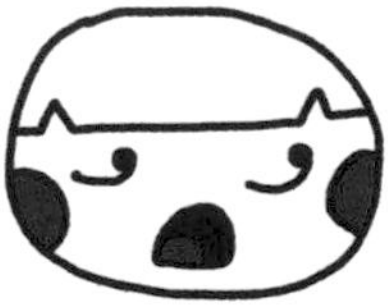

I'm sorry to cut this conversation short, but ______________________________.

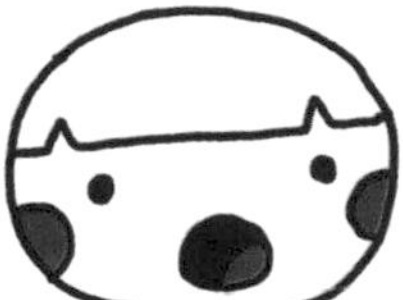

Oh, I missed your call! I couldn't hear the phone because ______________________________

______________________________.

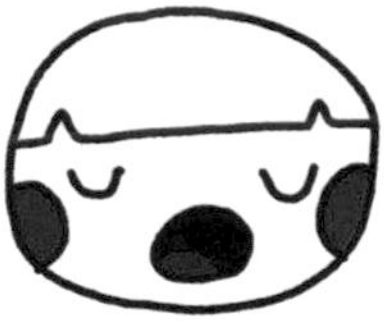

I PLANNED on going to your party, but then ____________________

______________________________.

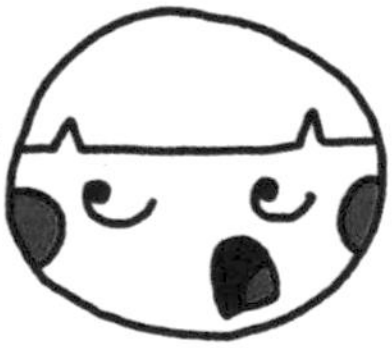

I'd love to hang out tonight! It's just, I've been experiencing some weird medical symptoms, like

____

____

____

CAREERS I'D BE GREAT AT

CAREERS I'D HATE

#80

PLAY WITH YOUR FOOD

GIVE US FACES

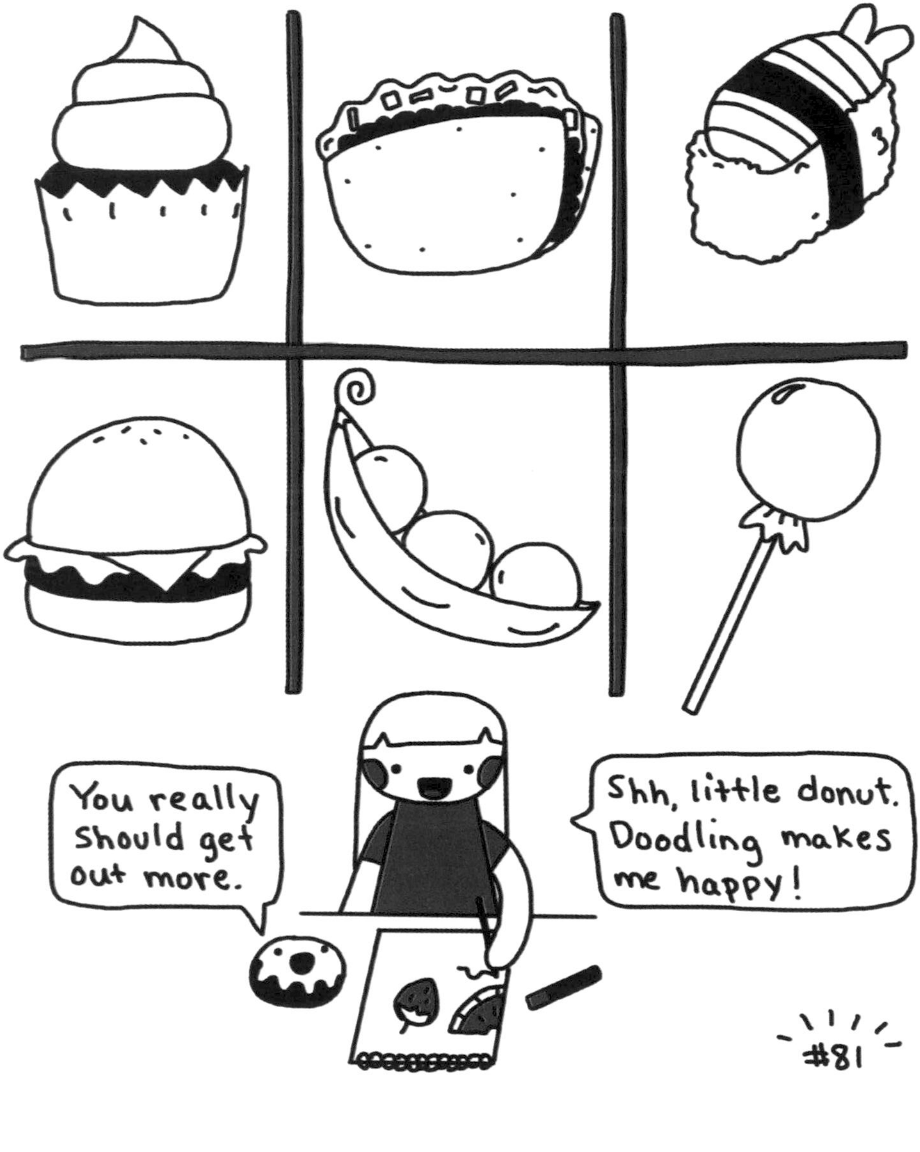
You really should get out more.
Shh, little donut. Doodling makes me happy!
#81

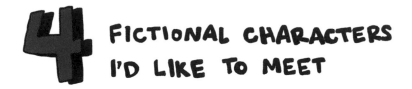

4 FICTIONAL CHARACTERS I'D LIKE TO MEET

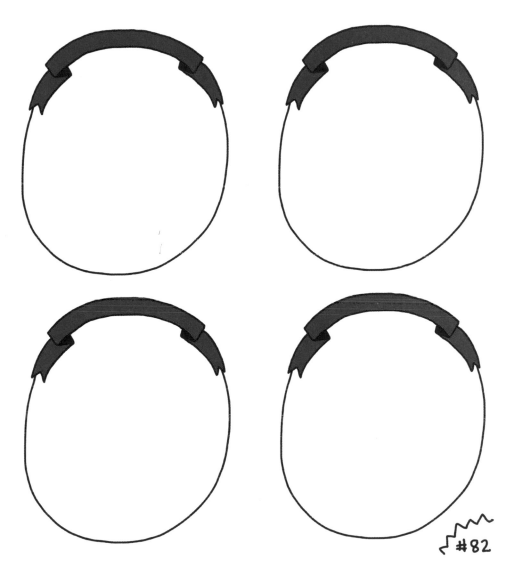

#82

CURATE A COLLECTION OF
COZY THINGS

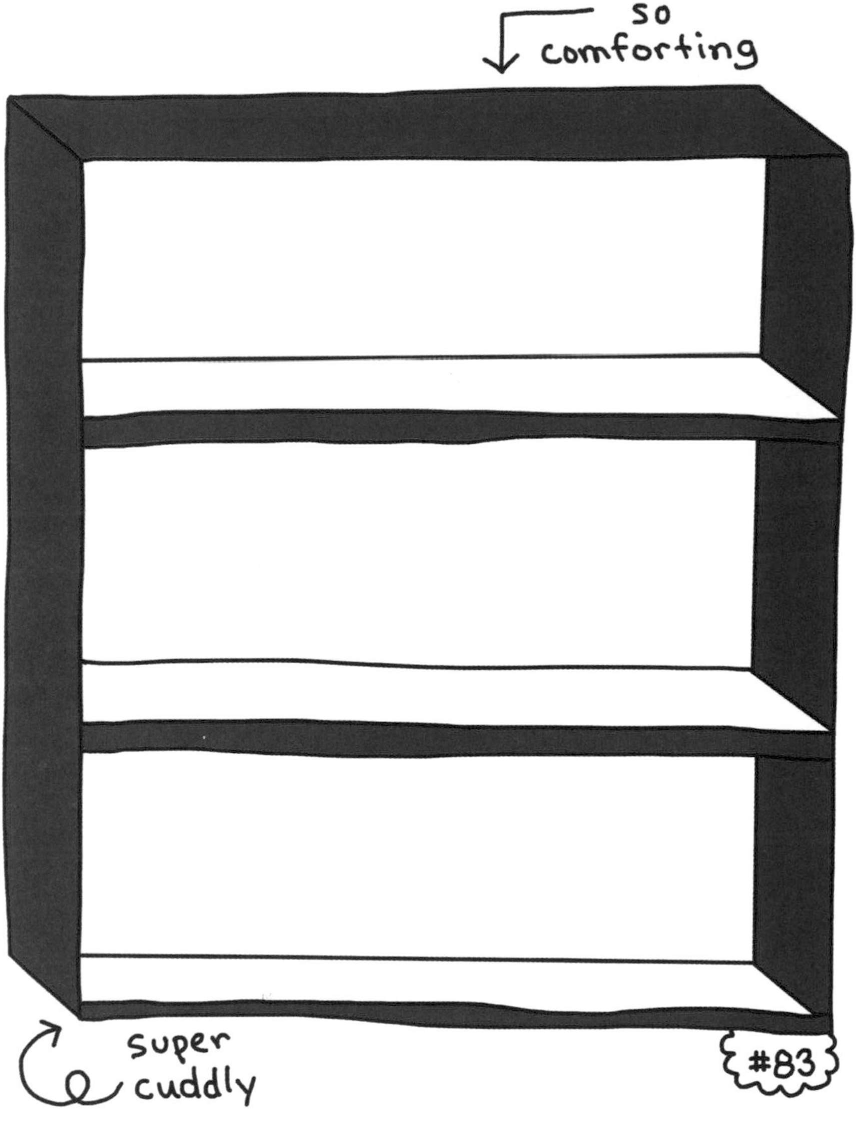
so comforting
super cuddly

#83

THIS PAGE LEFT BLANK.

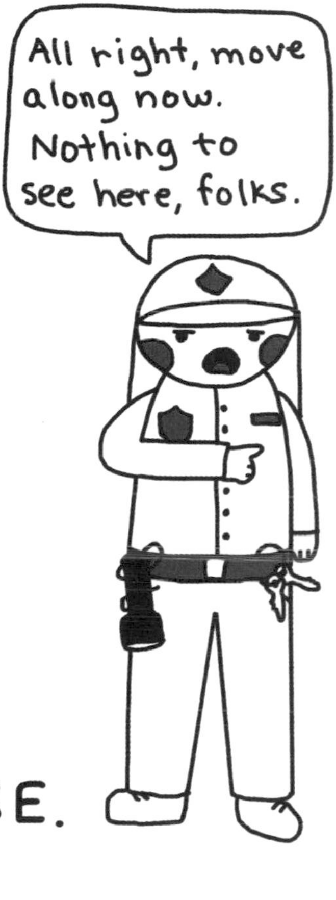
All right, move along now. Nothing to see here, folks.

ACTIVITY ON REVERSE.

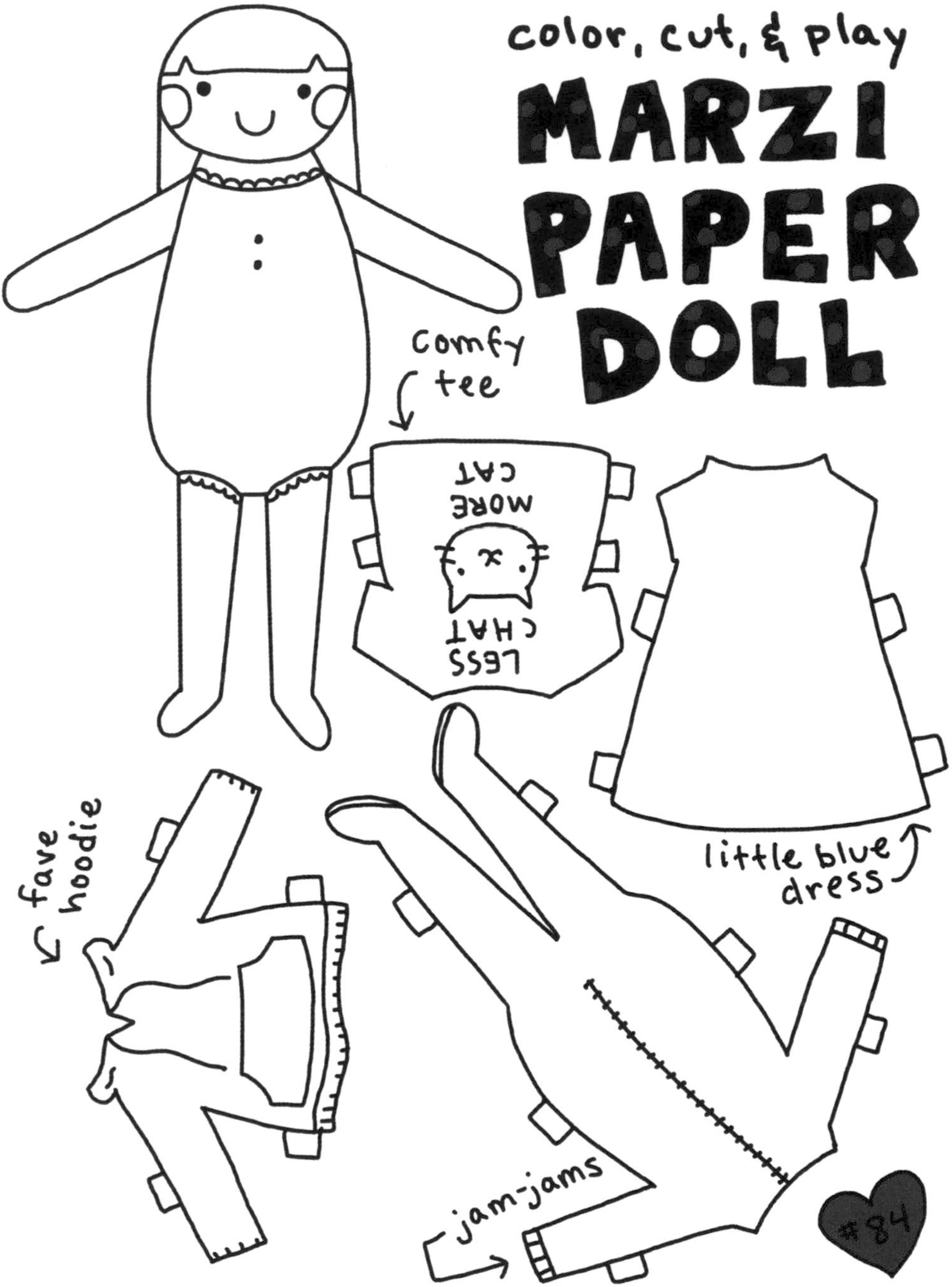
color, cut, & play
MARZI PAPER DOLL
comfy tee
LESS CHAT
MORE CAT
little blue dress
fave hoodie
jam-jams
#84

DUDES CAN BE INTROVERTS (AND DOLLS) TOO

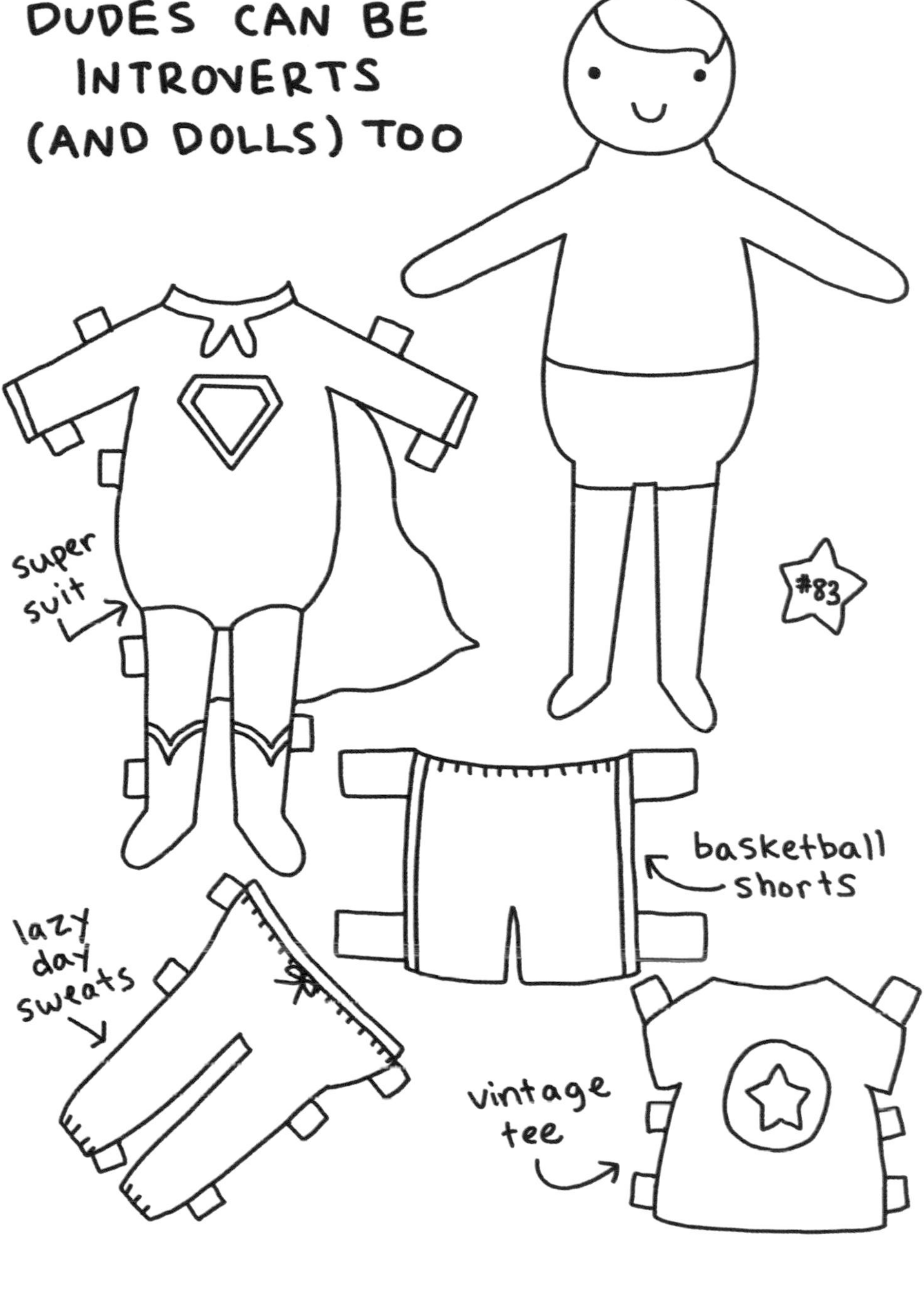
super suit
#83
basketball shorts
lazy day sweats
vintage tee

A picture of all my party clothes

Oh wait, I don't go to parties! Guess I'm gonna leave this page blank. It's gonna get cut up, anyways.

Bumper Stickers

IF YOU CAN READ THIS

THEN YOU'RE IN MY BUBBLE. BACK UP!

I'D ACTUALLY BUY!

Design a couple!

#85

RATE THESE FOODS

Shade in the bars below!

OATMEAL

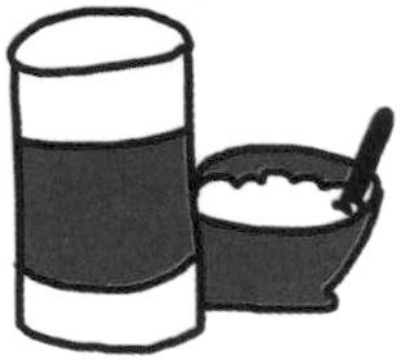

barf! icky meh tasty sooo good!

PIE

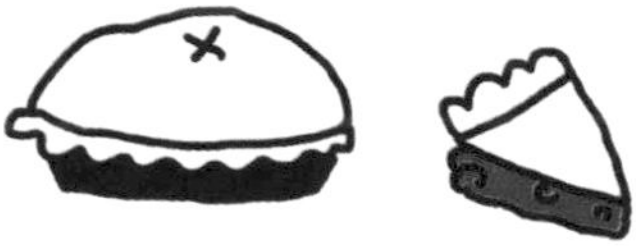

barf! icky meh tasty sooo good!

GUACAMOLE

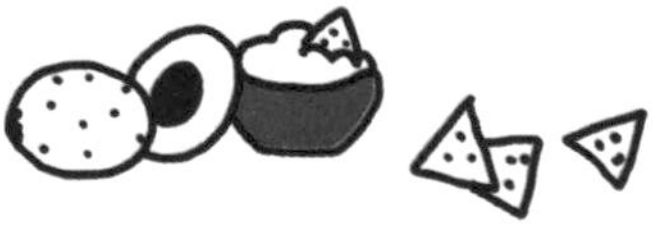

barf! icky meh tasty sooo good!

#86

PIZZA

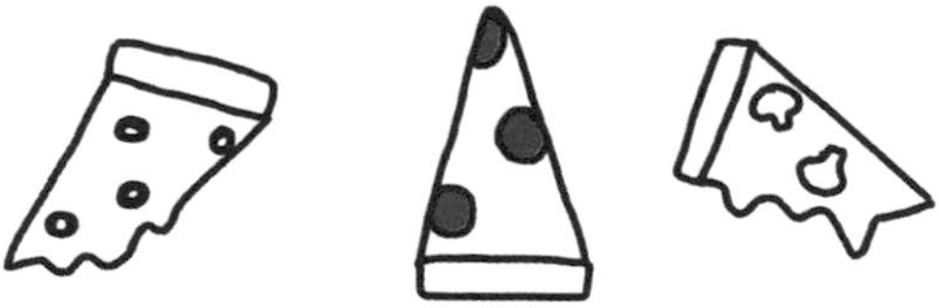

barf! icky meh tasty sooo good!

SALAD

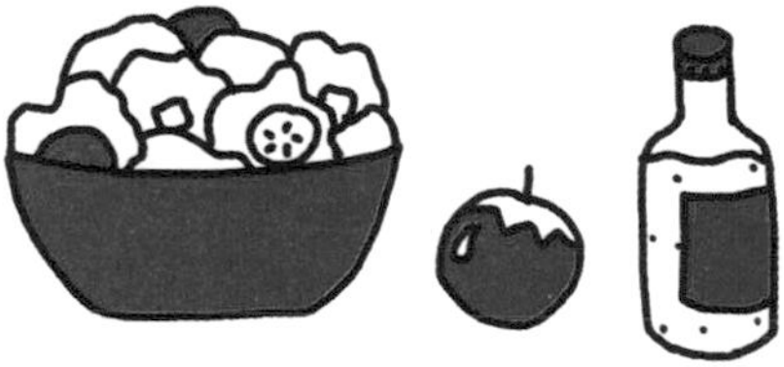

barf! icky meh tasty sooo good!

BLACK LICORICE

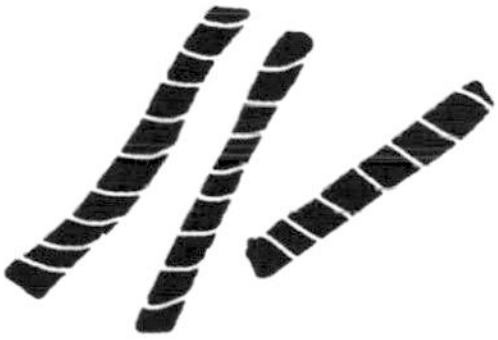

barf! icky meh tasty sooo good!

SEAFOOD

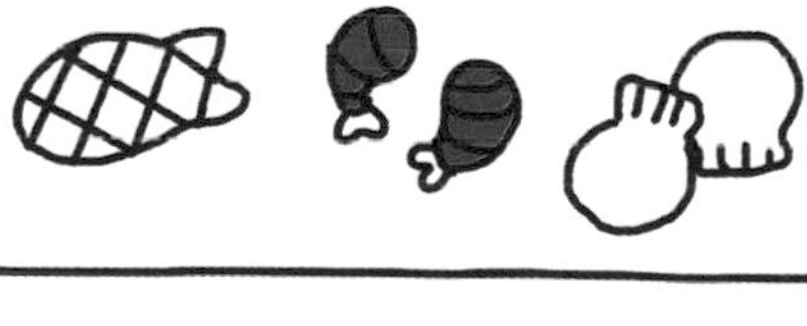

barf! icky meh tasty sooo good!

THE MOST *peaceful* PLACE I CAN *imagine...*

#87

I love the book "Quiet: The Power of Introverts in a World That Can't Stop Talking" by Susan Cain. It helped me recognize my hidden strengths! Now it's your turn...

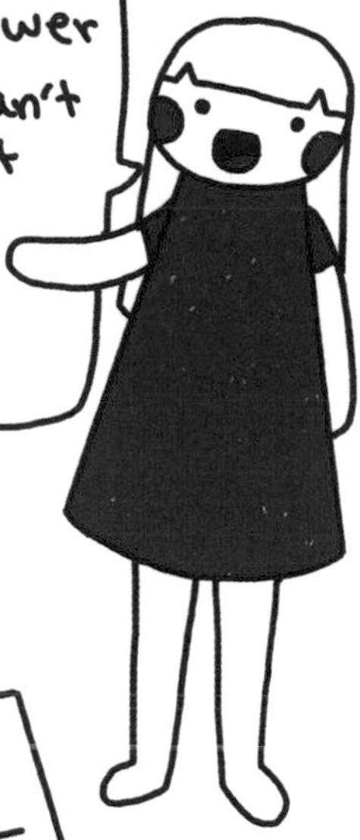

THIS BOOK CHANGED MY LIFE...

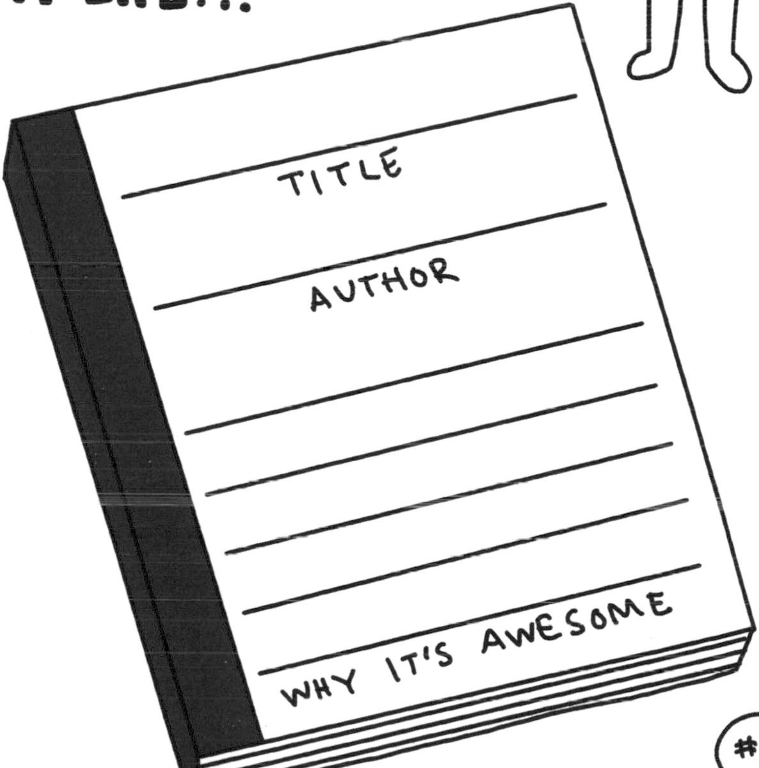
TITLE
AUTHOR
WHY IT'S AWESOME

#88

DOODLE LESSONS

PUG

Pizza slice ears

Eyebrows

CAT

squishy face

CACTUS

a little friend

so prickly

TRY IT!

~~~~~~

PUG

~~~~~~

CAT

~~~~~~

CACTUS

#89

MY RECENT BROWSING HISTORY

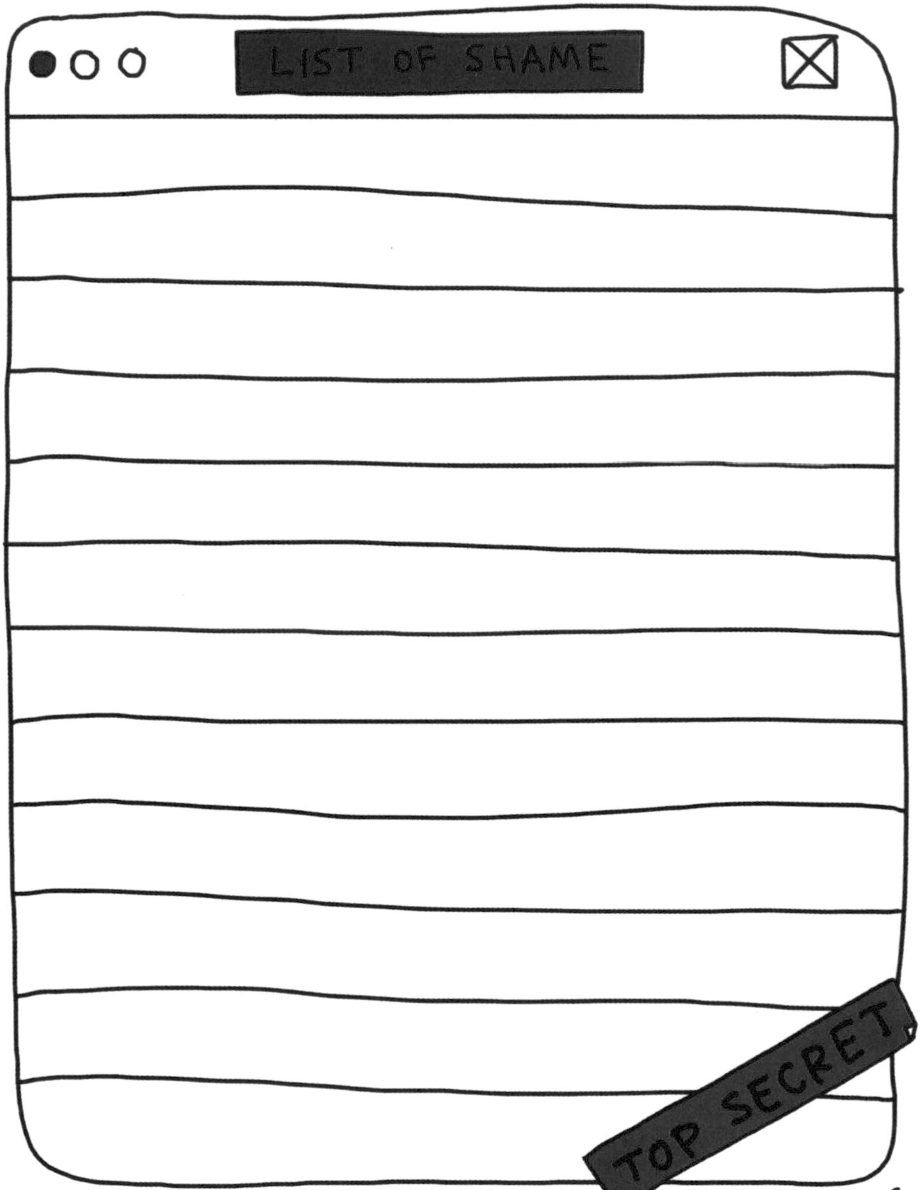
LIST OF SHAME
TOP SECRET

#90

DISGUISE THIS GUY

Hat? Hair? Beard? Bowtie? Make him mysterious!

#91

Love It -OR- HATE IT?

HOBBIES EDITION

COLOR THE ♡ OR THE 💔

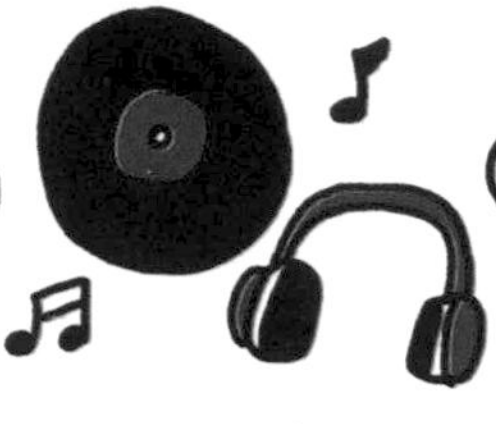

music

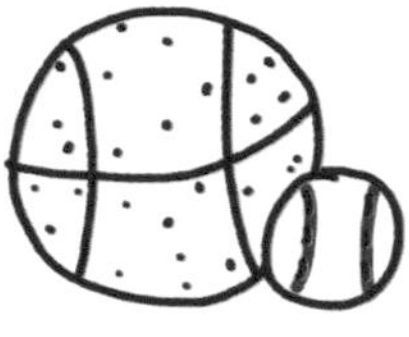

athletics

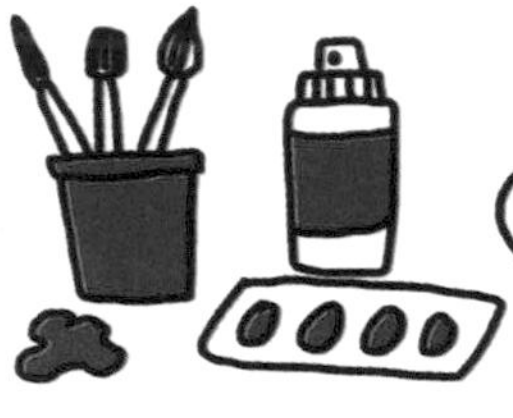

art

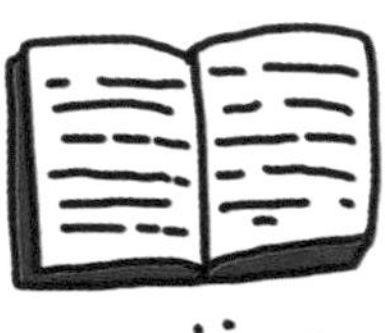

reading

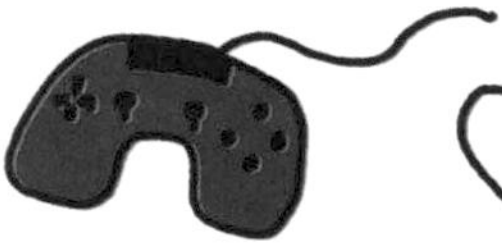

video games

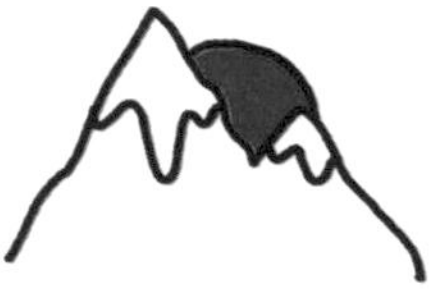

hiking

#92

TOP WAYS TO RECHARGE

doodle & label

#93

COLOR THESE AWKWARD SCENARIOS

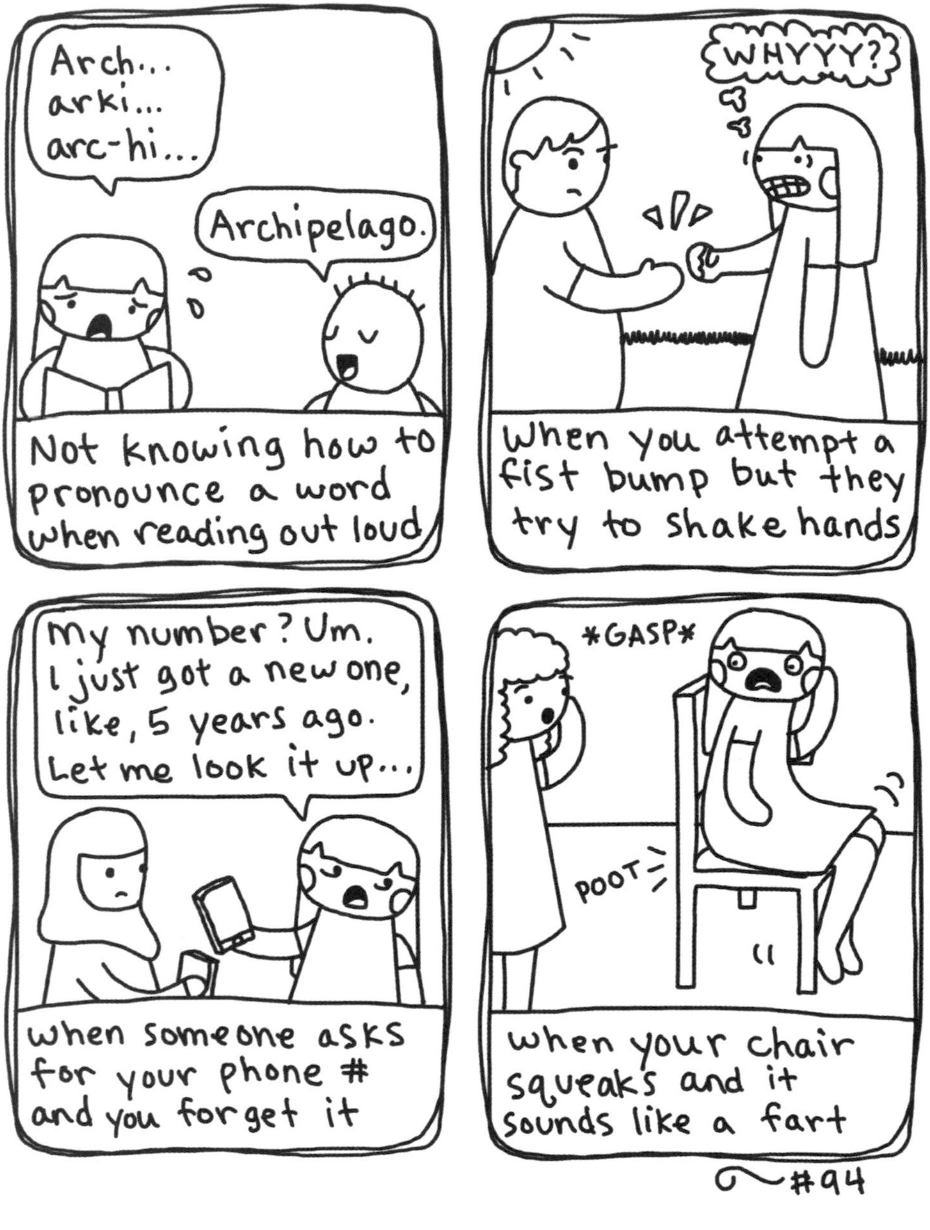

Arch... arki... arc-hi...
Archipelago.
Not knowing how to pronounce a word when reading out loud
WHYYY?
When you attempt a fist bump but they try to shake hands
My number? Um. I just got a new one, like, 5 years ago. Let me look it up...
when someone asks for your phone # and you forget it
GASP
POOT
when your chair squeaks and it sounds like a fart

#94

Separate the tabs on the dotted line.
Pin to a public bulletin board.

TAKE WHAT YOU NEED

Love | Coffee | Sleep | Energy | A smile | Understanding | More time | money | Hope

TAKE WHAT YOU NEED

create your own ↗

I know that tearing a page from a book goes against your core beliefs because you are a GOOD PERSON, but I'm gonna need you to go ahead and do it anyway. Just do it fast, like ripping off a Band-Aid. You can do this!

THIS PAGE LEFT BLANK

STUFF I CAN'T POSSIBLY LIVE WITHOUT

comfy pajamas

‡ #96 ‡

THIS VS. THAT

color your favorites

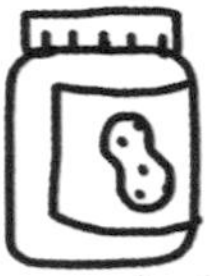

peanut butter

VS.

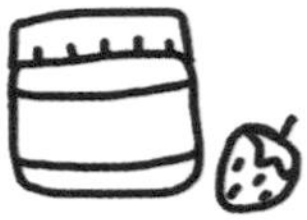

Nutella

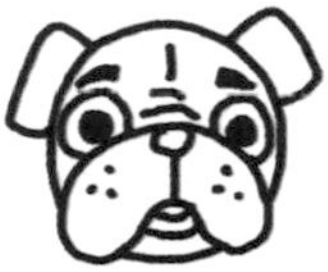

dogs

VS.

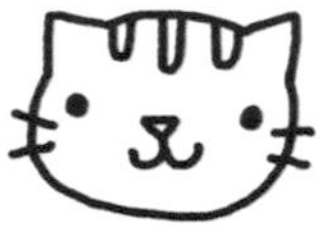

cats

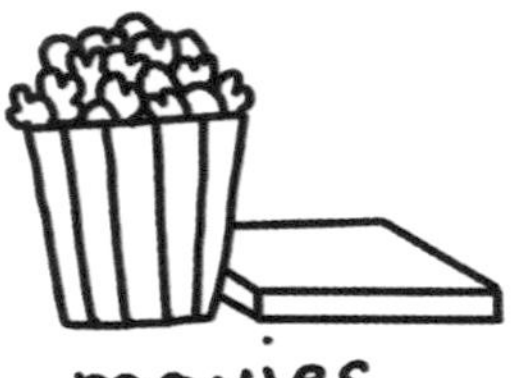

movies

VS.

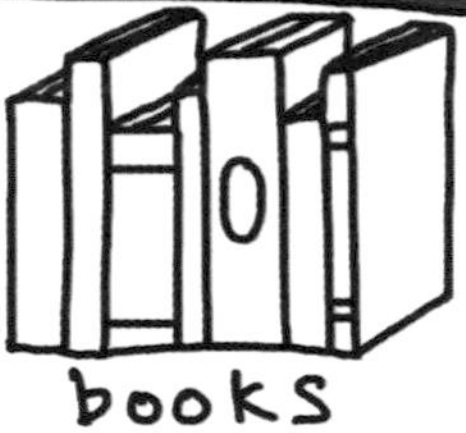

books

VS.

(make your own) ↗

#97

Design an INTROVERT WARDROBE

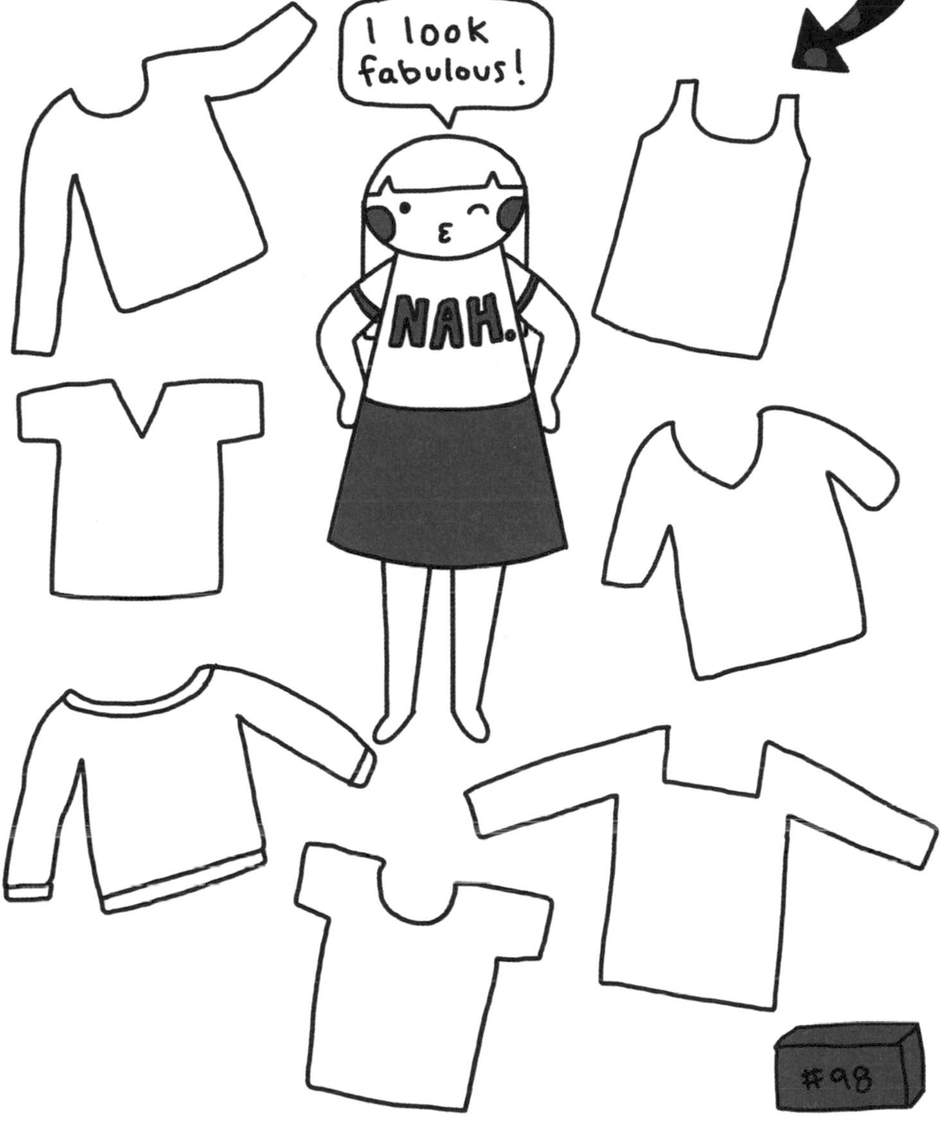
I look fabulous!
NAH.
#98

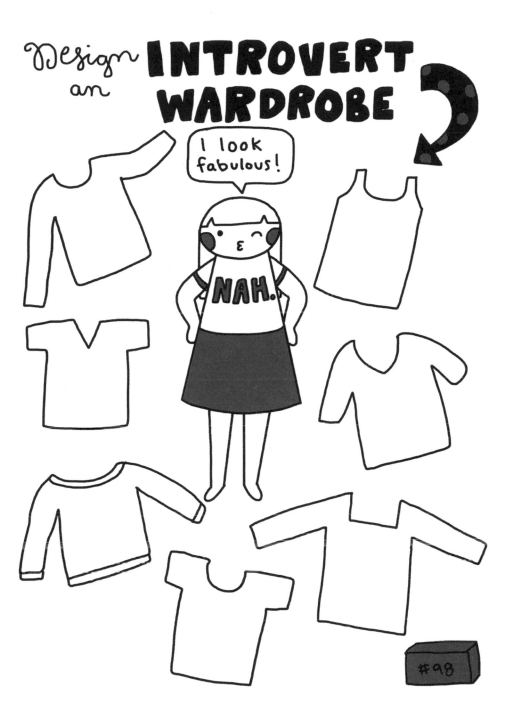

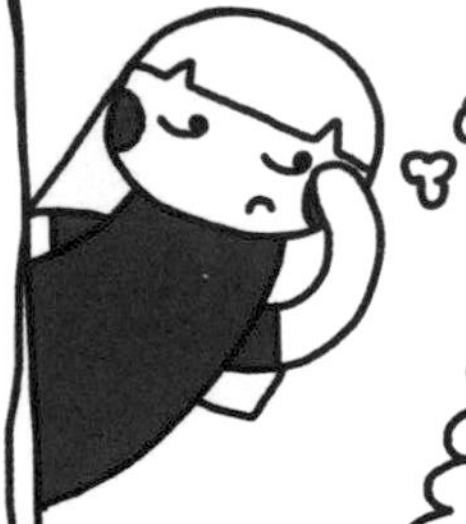

Stuff I worry about...

uh-oh

oh dear...

it could happen...

#99

DRAW AN EPIC FORT!

Include the following necessities:

- ☐ ball pit 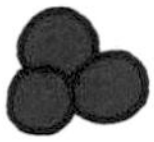
- ☐ hammock 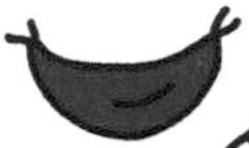
- ☐ slide 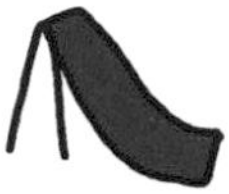
- ☐ rope ladder 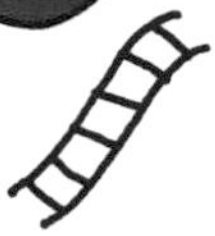

#100

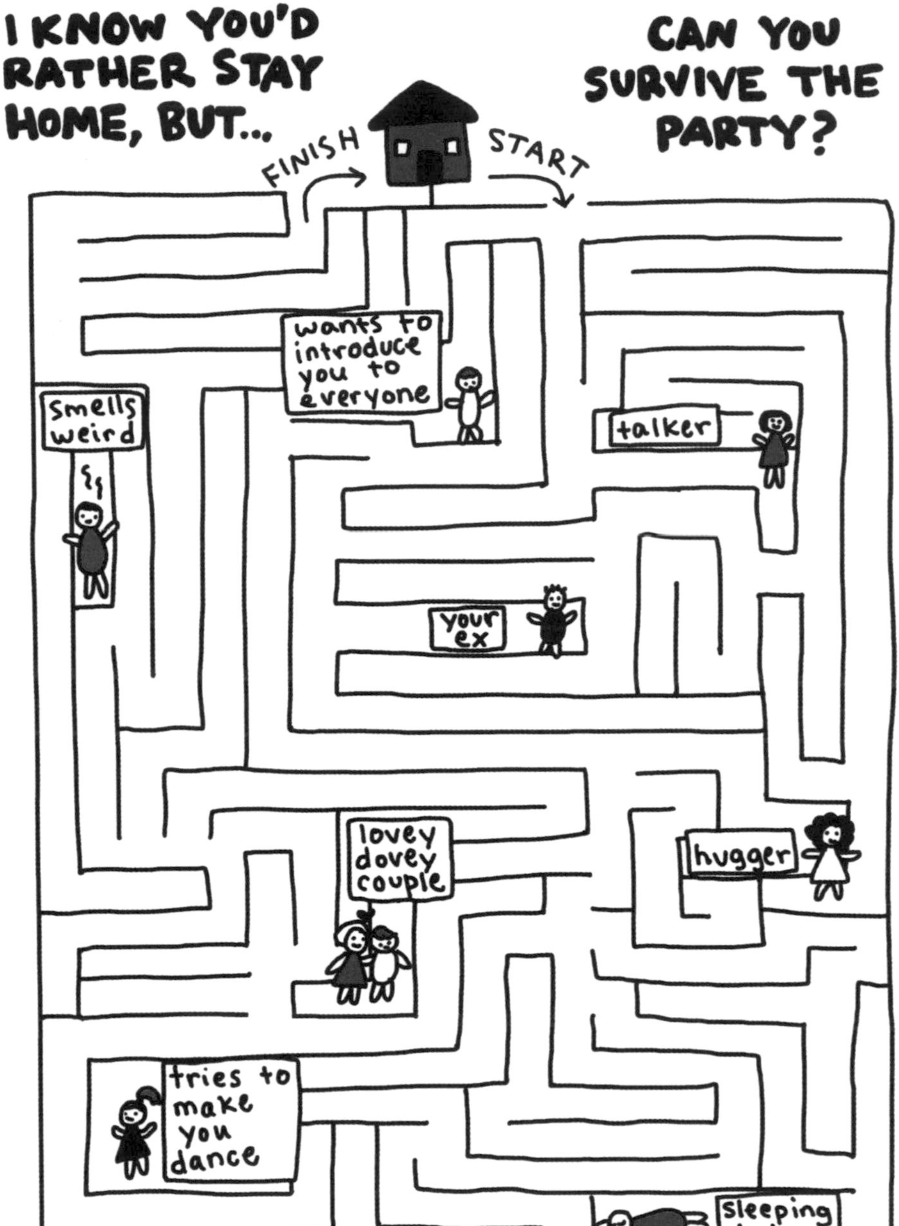
I KNOW YOU'D RATHER STAY HOME, BUT...
CAN YOU SURVIVE THE PARTY?
FINISH
START
wants to introduce you to everyone
smells weird
talker
your ex
hugger
lovey dovey couple
tries to make you dance
sleeping dude

#101

GUILTY Pleasures

 5

 4

 3

 2

 1

#Sorrynotsorry

#102

BINGE-WORTHY SHOWS

Fav character

Name:

Rating: ☆☆☆☆☆

Why it's good:

Fav character

Name:

Rating: ☆☆☆☆☆

Why it's good:

Fav character

Name:

Rating: ☆☆☆☆☆

Why it's good:

#103

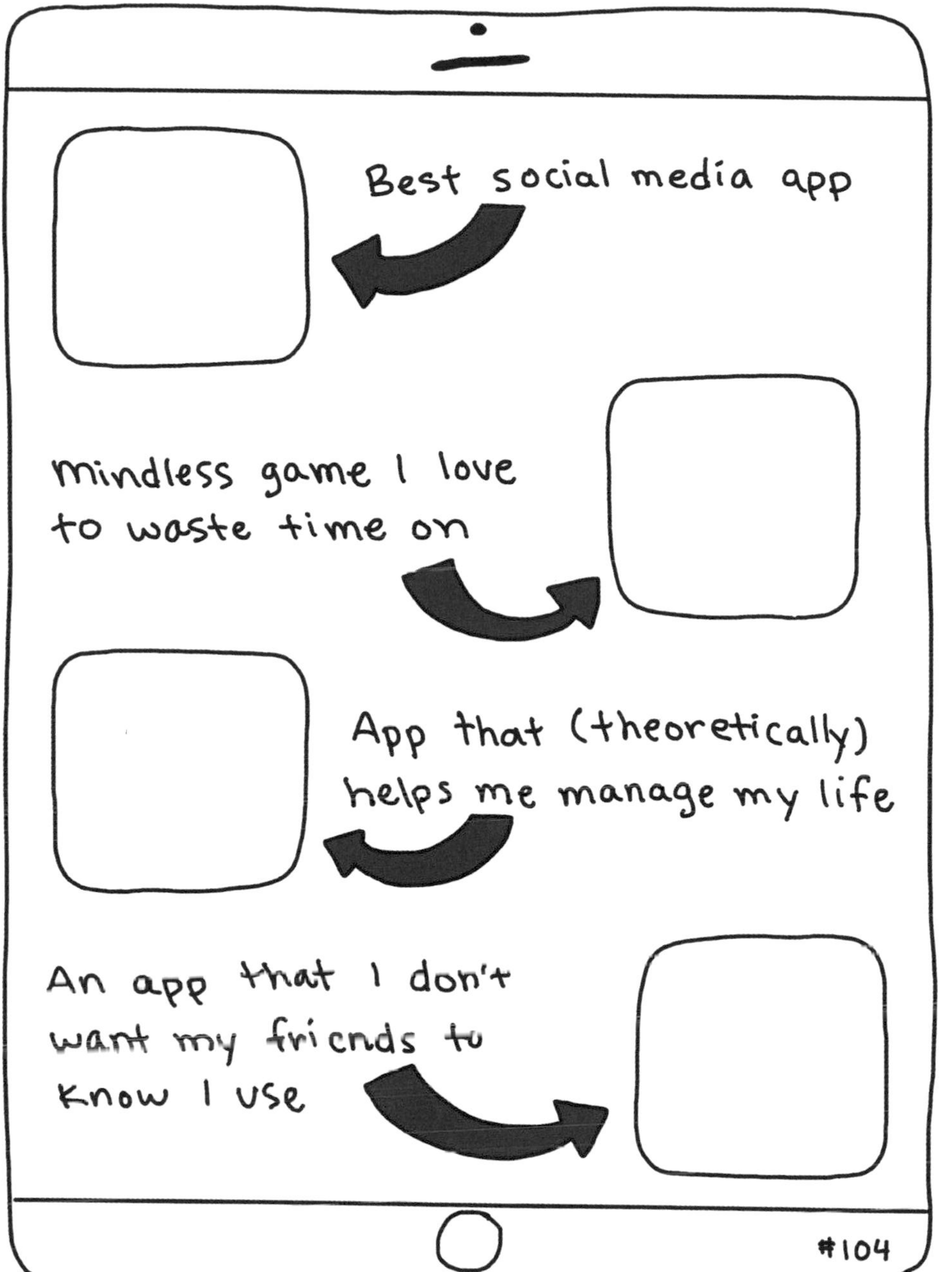
Best social media app
mindless game I love to waste time on
App that (theoretically) helps me manage my life
An app that I don't want my friends to know I use
#104

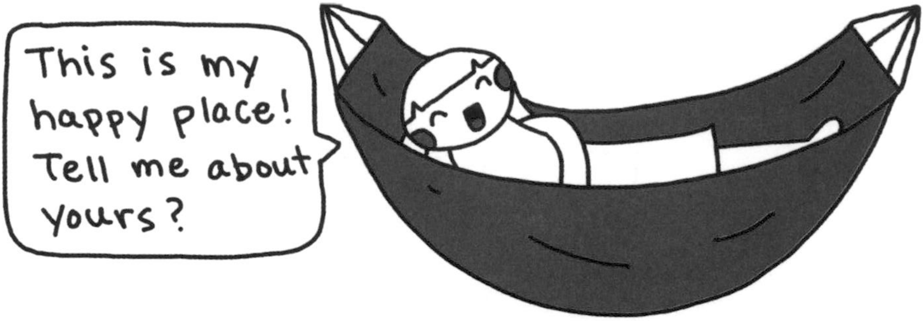
This is my happy place! Tell me about yours?

MY FAVORITE PLACES

To eat:

To nap:

To read:

To think:

To create:

To hang out:

To vacation:

To enjoy nature:

#105

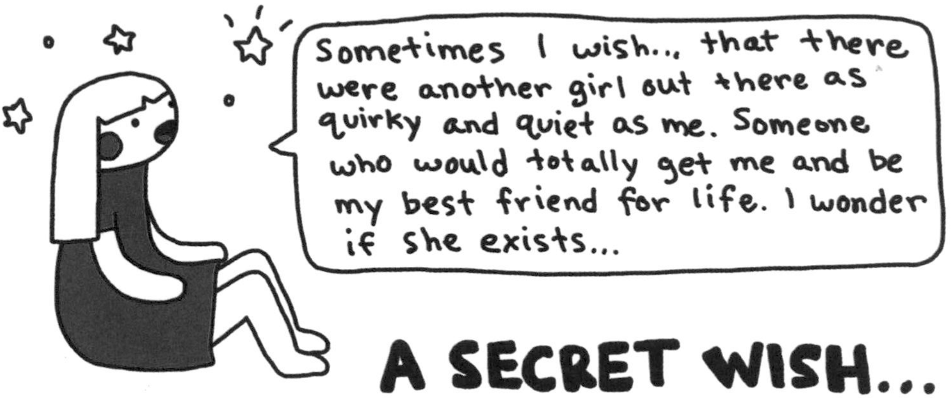
Sometimes I wish... that there were another girl out there as quirky and quiet as me. Someone who would totally get me and be my best friend for life. I wonder if she exists...

A SECRET WISH...

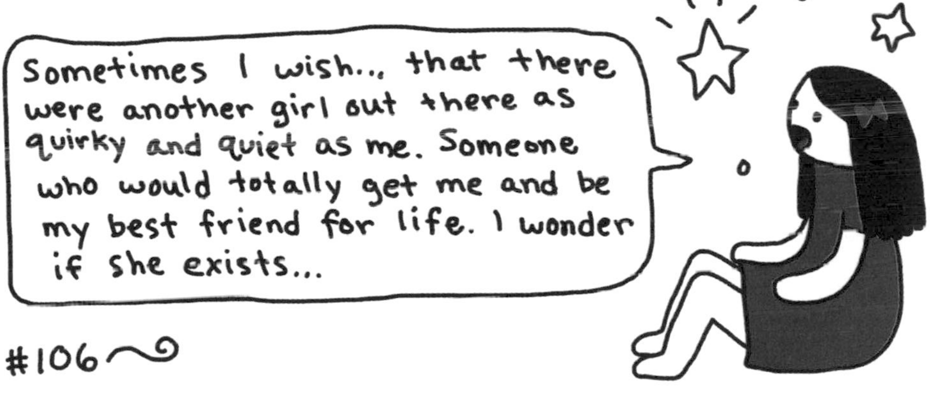
Sometimes I wish... that there were another girl out there as quirky and quiet as me. Someone who would totally get me and be my best friend for life. I wonder if she exists...

#106

THINGS I'M TIRED OF HEARING

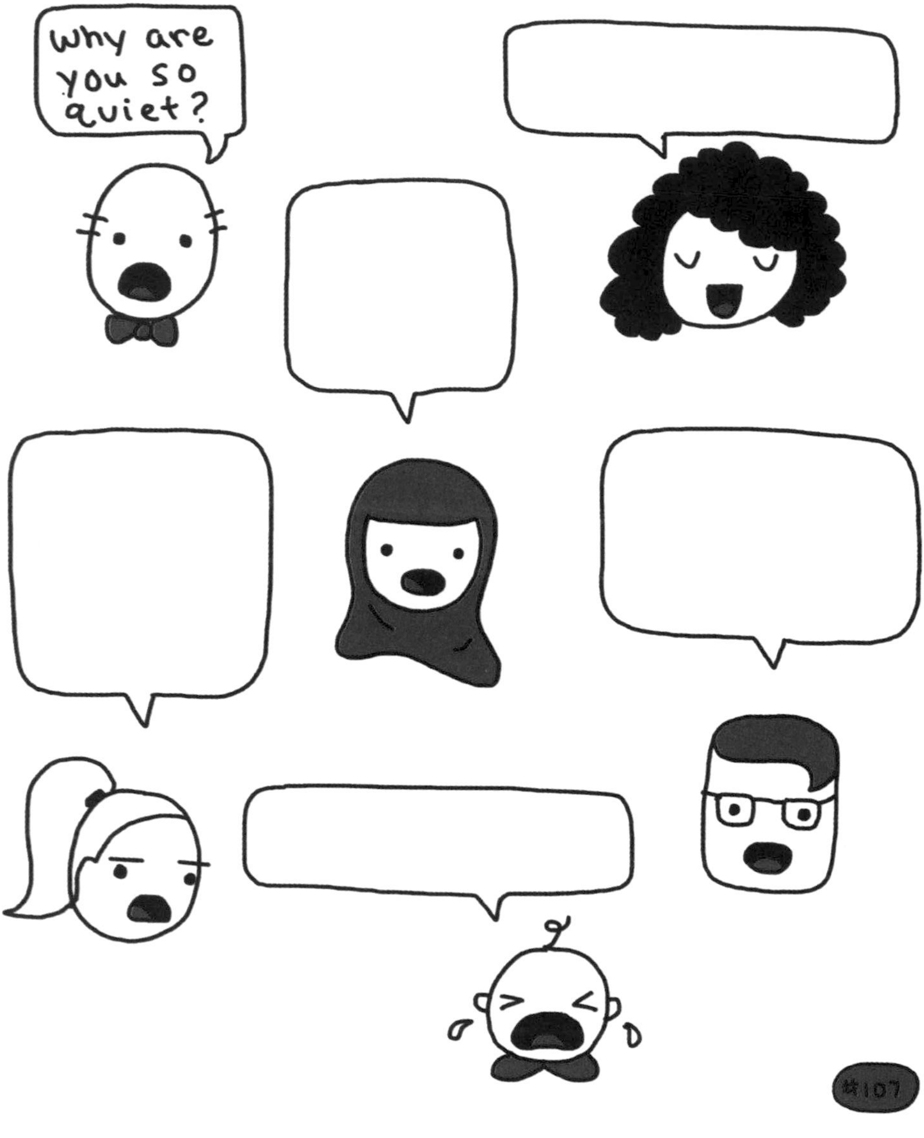
Why are you so quiet?

#107

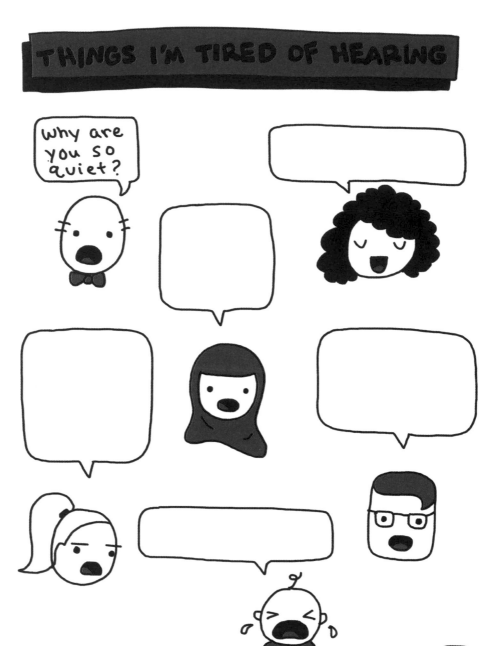

TIME FOR A CLOSE-UP

How detail-oriented are you? See if you can identify the close-up details within this book!

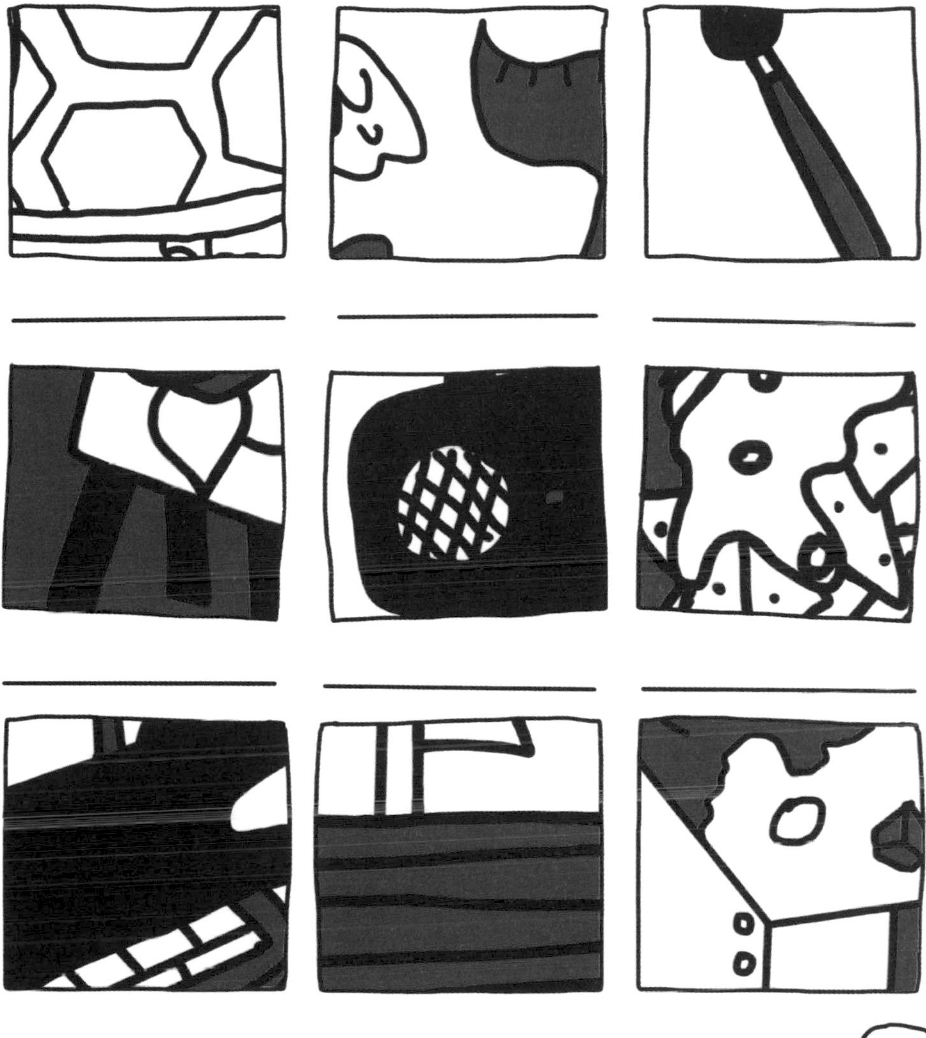

#108

ABOUT THE AUTHOR (THAT'S ME!)

Name/nickname:

_____

Current location:

_____

Social media username:

_____

Interesting fact:

_____

_____

Accomplishments:

_____

_____

X

Autograph

#109

...BUT I LET MARZI HELP A LITTLE

Name/nickname:

Maureen Marzi Wilson

Current location:

middle of nowhere, USA

Social media username:

@introvertdoodles

Interesting fact:

Does not actually own a little blue dress.

Loves the smell of skunks (truly!)

Accomplishments:

author of "Introvert Doodles: an Illustrated

Look at Introvert Life in an Extrovert World"

x

XOXO, Marzi

Autograph

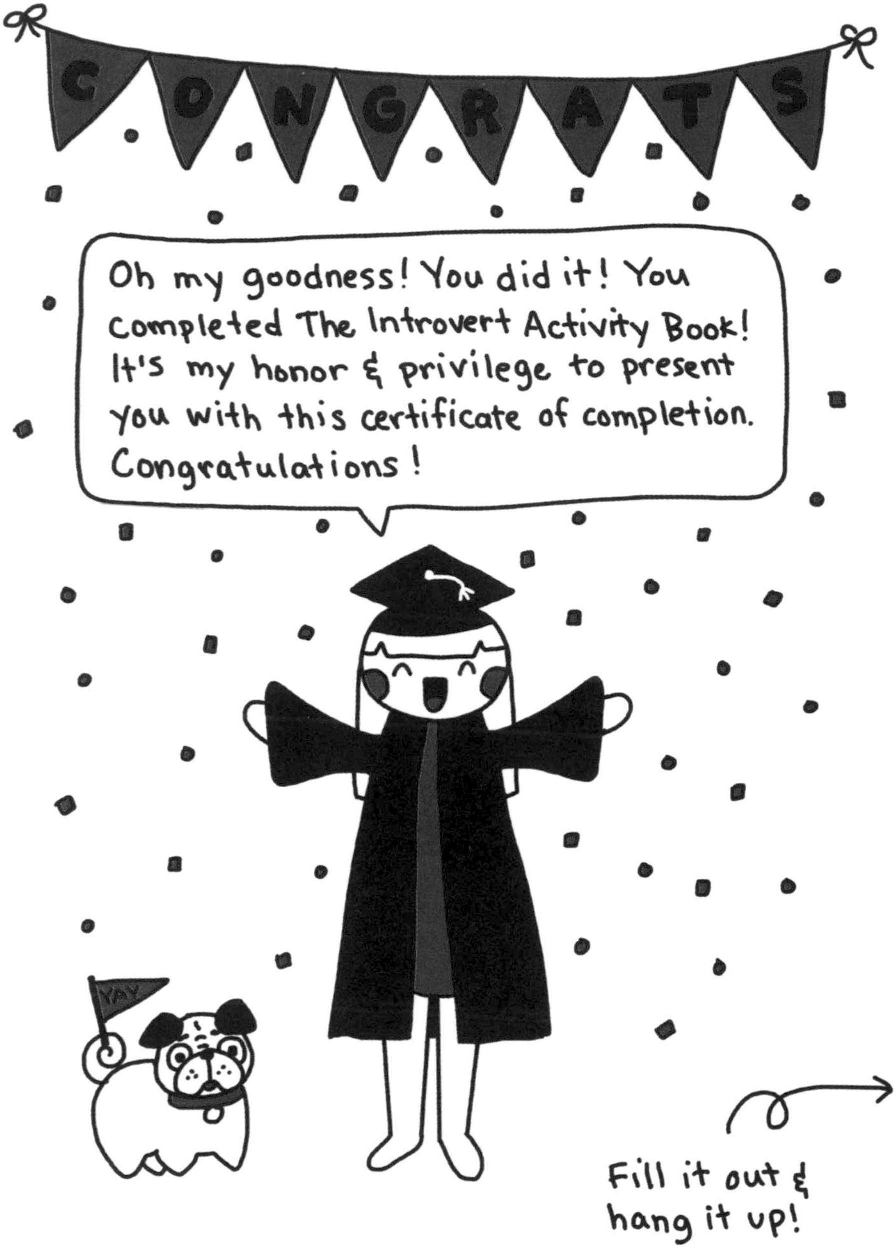
CONGRATS
Oh my goodness! You did it! You completed The Introvert Activity Book! It's my honor & privilege to present you with this certificate of completion. Congratulations!
YAY
Fill it out & hang it up!

Certificate of Completion

Awarded to

_____

an introvert of the highest caliber, for the successful completion of

THE
INTROVERT
ACTIVITY
BOOK

Date: _____

#110